Mark Anthony the Psychic Lawyer®
Redefines Spirit Contact,
Bringing It Into the Twenty-First Century

Discover the enlightening and comforting true stories of
Mark Anthony the Psychic Lawyer® as he helps people communicate with their loved ones in spirit. *Evidence of Eternity*
is an uplifting journey that removes the fear and superstition
surrounding spirit contact while addressing poignant questions about the afterlife. It provides insights on painful subjects such as crime, homicide, suicide, and survivor guilt.

By bridging the gap between the spiritual and scientific,
this groundbreaking book brings spirit communication into
the modern era while reaffirming that God and heaven exist,
the soul is an immortal living spirit, and that we will be reunited with our deceased loved ones.

Evidence of Eternity introduces new and innovative terms
and concepts explaining spirit communication based on science, theoretical physics, physiology, theology, and evidence.
From karma and reincarnation to embracing the inner light,
Evidence of Eternity is a cutting-edge perspective of life after
death.

EVIDENCE *of* •
eternity

Mark Anthony the Psychic Lawyer® is a world-renowned fourth-generation psychic medium who specializes in communication with spirits. He is an Oxford-educated attorney and certified mediator licensed to practice law in Florida; Washington, DC; and before the United States Supreme Court. He has also studied mediumship at the prestigious Arthur Findlay College for the Advancement of Psychic Science.

Mark appears worldwide on radio and TV as a psychic medium legal analyst in high-profile murder cases and as a paranormal expert. He regularly appears on ABC, CBS, NBC, FOX Television, Coast to Coast AM, Darkness Radio, Fox News Talk, CBS Radio, ABC Radio, and Sirius XM Radio. Mark Anthony is a featured speaker at conventions, grief support groups, hospice organizations, conferences, expos, spiritual organizations such as the Edgar Cayce Association for Research and Enlightenment, and universities including Harvard, Brown, and Yale.

For more information about Mark Anthony, please visit www.EvidenceOfEternity.com.

EVIDENCE *of* •
eternity

Communicating with Spirits
for Proof of the Afterlife

MARK
ANTHONY

THE PSYCHIC LAWYER®

Llewellyn Publications
WOODBURY, MINNESOTA

FIRST EDITION
First Printing, 2015

Book design by Rebecca Zins
Cover image © iStockphoto.com/30066262/©Vladimir Arndt
Cover design by Ellen Lawson

Llewellyn Publications is a registered trademark
of Llewellyn Worldwide Ltd.

Library of Congress Cataloging-in-Publication Data
Anthony, Mark, 1960–
  Evidence of eternity : communicating with spirits for proof of the afterlife
/ Mark Anthony.—first edition.
     pages cm
  ISBN 978-0-7387-4388-2
1. Spiritualism. 2. Future life. I. Title.
  BF1272.A57 2015
  133.9'1—dc23

                                                    2014039185

Llewellyn Publications
A Division of Llewellyn Worldwide Ltd.
2143 Wooddale Drive
Woodbury, MN 55125-2989
www.llewellyn.com

Printed in the United States of America

This book is dedicated to my father, Earl, the bravest man I have ever known. He served his country not only in a time of war but in times of peace by expanding our understanding of the universe through space exploration.

I also dedicate this book to his fellow veterans and to all of the brave men and women of the United States Armed Forces who defend our right to freedom of speech and freedom of belief.

Contents

Contents

Foreword

As a researcher of near-death experiences (NDEs), I never wanted to have that much to do with mediums, particularly during the early stages of my career. My work with near-death experiences and my interest in UFO experiences was outré enough for an academic like me. Besides, I was never interested in trying to prove life after death, anyway, or even make a good case for survival of consciousness after physical death. I was always more interested in showing what we could learn from near-death experiences and letting my students and readers draw whatever conclusions they liked. For an academic to get too close to mediums and talk about the afterlife was to court banishment from the academy—it was stuff for the tabloids, not for the halls of ivy.

However, during my years of researching altered states of consciousness and NDEs, I learned a lot about mediums. I have no doubt that some of them can indeed transmit messages from the dead and know things about the people they are reading for that would be impossible to know by normal means. And naturally, I had read about many of the celebrated mediums of the past—Leonora Piper, Gladys Osborne Leonard, and many others. Yet I never sought out a reading for myself until a couple of years ago, when something very peculiar happened to me that, in the end, I could not ignore. Ultimately, it proved to have something to do with my father.

When I was very young, I was separated from my father when he went off to war during the early 1940s. Although he survived the war, for various reasons he never returned home, and then he died young, at forty-one, while working as an artist in New York. As I grew to manhood, I started thinking a lot about my father and began to sense his presence in my life as a kind of guiding influence. As a scientist, my initial reaction was to question this sensation, but on some level I felt the connection was real, so I decided to write a memoir about my father and his putative effect on my life after his death; I called it *My Father, Once Removed*.

Then, two years ago, I started to hear from a number of my friends—all of them independently of one another and all of them connected in some way with NDE studies—who had recently had some kind of fantastic reading from a medium (never the same medium, mind you) and who were asking me if I ever had considered having a reading myself. Most of them exhorted me to. Of course I demurred, declined, and generally deflected the conversation to other topics—except it *kept happening*!

After the fourth such occurrence, I finally succumbed and arranged for a reading with one of the mediums who had been urged upon me by one of these friends. Afterward I wrote an article about my reading entitled, somewhat humorously, "Medium Hot," which I eventually inserted as the last chapter into a revised and expanded version of my memoir about my father.

I will spare you the details, but the reading I received strongly and independently corroborated virtually everything I had learned or speculated about my father's life, which the medium could not have known by normal means. And not only that, the medium stressed my father's feelings of deep love for me, which I had previously learned from his half sister, as well as his posthumous role in my life, which I had long sensed. Moreover, the medium was accurately able to tell me some extremely obscure facts about my family life that really blew me away. It's one thing to read about such things in books; it's quite another when it happens to you!

In any case, it became apparent to me that science and mediumship are not mutually exclusive, especially when the medium focuses on evidence that can be objectively verified. This is why I have found what Mark Anthony has observed about the Other Side to be very instructive. His observations are based on a logical, scientific approach, rooted in evidence and not on suppositions or jumping to conclusions. This, indeed, is one of the facets of *Evidence of Eternity* that I find impressive. Mark takes great care to demonstrate why it is important not to bring one's expectations of negativity or fear into the explorations of spirits or normally invisible entities. Of course, the unknown is often frightening, just as the night is, but his accounts of contact with spirits are very telling in this respect, as well as fascinating in their own right.

Mark approaches spirit communication with integrity and professionalism. Despite his rigorous approach to his work, because he gives public demonstrations of communication with spirits, a lawyer who speaks with the dead is certainly not immune from ridicule. However, based on his sense of humor, the integrity with which he approaches his spiritual work, and, most importantly, his faith in God, it seems he often has the last laugh! For my part, although I have sometimes had rewarding and stimulating encounters with true skeptics, I find debunkers masquerading as skeptics to be tedious since they have imprisoned themselves within the walls of their own ideology, so I tend to give such people a wide berth.

There are many points of resonance and consistency between Mark's work and the research on NDEs. The fascinating aspect of *Evidence of Eternity* is that messages from the Other Side take up the story after the NDE trail goes cold, but the two fit together like the proverbial hand and glove. Perhaps even more significant is that the spiritual implications both for living in this world (in terms of the values by which one should live) and for the existence of an afterlife coincide with accounts of NDE research.

The big questions, of course, are what happens after death, and what is the Other Side like? Many who study life after death, including Mark, theorize that the Other Side has different levels, if one might put it that way, and that people are naturally attracted to the levels that are appropriate to them. There appears to be a consensus that there is no such thing as an archetypal hell, which is something that people who have a near-death experience would agree with. Still another point Mark's observations have in common with NDE research has to do with reincarnation. In my research (and in some other work on NDEs), I found that many NDEers became more open to the idea of reincarnation following their NDE, and quite a few of them came to believe in some form of it.

Mark Anthony touches upon many sensitive issues in *Evidence of Eternity*, including suicide. From the standpoint of NDE research, generally speaking, my coinvestigators and I found that people who attempt suicide have the same kind of initial experience as do people who have NDEs through illness or accident: they encounter the Light, too, and all the love that is associated with it. Nevertheless, they understand that suicide would have solved nothing, and that they would still have to work through the same issues. Indeed, in a certain sense, it is impossible to kill yourself because even when your body dies, you find that you are still alive. So, virtually all such people return knowing that suicide is not the answer. It's more complicated than that, of course, but Mark's reports of individuals who have committed suicide coincide with what I have found through my NDE research.

Another point of congruence between Mark's work and the findings of NDEs is that one's individuality is never lost, even when it becomes a part of something much larger. Nevertheless, one retains a sense of one's own personality when one becomes a spirit, just as Mark has observed. I have heard the same thing maintained by NDEers I have interviewed.

Thus, Mark Anthony's work leads to very much the same set of implications for how to live as does the research on NDEs, plus it goes further than NDE studies by giving the reader a clear sense that we are never separated from our loved ones and of what life after the death of the body is like.

I also thoroughly enjoyed reading about Mark's views on animals in the afterlife, as NDEers sometimes also report encountering their deceased pets during their NDE. Then, too, the humor in the book was delightful, giving it charm as well as depth.

On a more serious matter, as Mark indicates and as NDE studies show, we find that we are responsible for our actions here and will reap the consequences of them later, even after death. However, I want to make it clear that during the life review portion of an NDE, there is no judgment and no sense of punishment as such. Instead, one simply sees the effects of one's actions on those affected by them—and experiences them as if these actions also affected oneself. Thus, there is a sense of perfect justice—what one reaps, one truly does sow. One sees immediately that the Golden Rule is not merely a precept for moral behavior; it is the way it works. Here again, there is, I believe, another point of strong resonance with *Evidence of Eternity*.

Perhaps the most important parallel between Mark's work and NDE studies, however, is the conclusion that one's life is eternal. The Light of divinity exists within all of us, and this realization removes the fear of the unknown regarding what happens after we die. Life does not cease to exist when the body dies; Mark's work points to the inescapable conclusion that we have a soul that is connected to a greater consciousness that continues to live in spirit form in another dimension—a realm where a higher intelligence of unconditional love exists to welcome us home when our time comes to live elsewhere.

Kenneth Ring

Professor Emeritus of Psychology, University of Connecticut, author of the *New York Times* bestseller *Lessons from the Light*

Introduction

Since the dawn of recorded history, millions of people worldwide have reported contact with spirits of deceased loved ones. Despite the prevalence of spirit communication, many people refuse to believe in it or are skeptical of it or feel it is somehow negative. Due to the superstition and fear surrounding spirit contact, many are reluctant to admit even having such an experience. However, attitudes are changing, and today millions of people seek connection with deceased loved ones through mediums.

In my work as a psychic medium, I facilitate communication between people here in the material world and spirits of deceased loved ones. I am both an attorney and a psychic medium and am known as Mark Anthony the Psychic Lawyer®. While many people tend to think of my two professions as polar opposites, they are actually both about evidence, and this book is about evidence received from the afterlife.

People want to know: What happens when I die? Is there an afterlife? Does heaven exist? Does hell exist? Do animals have souls? What do messages from spirits mean? How can spirit communication help me? Is reincarnation real? Can you communicate with the spirit of someone who has already reincarnated? What if I die and my loved one has already reincarnated; does that mean I'll never see her again, even on the Other Side?

Other questions arise as well: Is there any science to prove this? Does the devil exist? My son committed suicide; did he go to hell? The man who murdered my grandfather was found not guilty; if there is a God, how could God allow that?

This book addresses these questions and removes the fear and superstition surrounding spirit contact. My approach is to bridge the gap between the spiritual and the scientific. In this book I explain how science and faith are not mutually exclusive; in fact, they're often in harmony. Quantum physics, physiology, genetics, scientific theory, history, and theology are woven together in an engaging style that presents the scientific basis and theories concerning life after death, spirit communication (both human and animal), karma, reincarnation, enlightenment, and what I call "inlightenment" (each individual's personal connection with God).

Through this logical approach, the book reaffirms for the reader that God exists, heaven exists, the soul is an immortal living spirit, communication with spirits is possible, and that we will be reunited with our deceased loved ones again once it is our time to leave this life. Yet it goes further than other books of this genre because it takes these truths to a much deeper level and brings the reality of the afterlife and spirit contact to the reader in a new way.

Evidence of Eternity explains innovative, complex, and esoteric concepts in easy-to-understand language. Inspirational, gripping, edgy, and occasionally humorous true stories drive each chapter to educate, entertain, enlighten, and console the reader. Healing is a major component of this book, which tackles the tough, painful topic of the death of a loved one.

This book brings life after death into the twenty-first century by redefining the understanding of the afterlife and the technical aspects of spirit communication. These new terms and concepts are introduced in a logical and progressive manner in order to build upon other new concepts presented in subsequent chapters.

I was raised as a Catholic and even considered entering the clergy. Even though I chose a career in law, I've spent my life studying God and the religions of the world. By the term

God I am referring to belief in a Higher Power. Humanity has given a host of names to this Higher Power, such as Supreme Being, Yahweh, Christ, Brahman, Vishnu, Buddha, Jehovah, Allah, Great Spirit, Holy Spirit, the Source, and Infinite Light. I choose to simply refer to the Higher Power as God.

Evidence of Eternity is for all people of all faiths. It is impossible to talk about life after death without discussing God and how the major world religions have viewed God, the nature of heaven or the Other Side, reincarnation, and communication with spirits. The ultimate objective of science may quite possibly be the discovery of God. To that end, understanding the technology behind spirituality and how to interpret the evidence transmitted to us by spirits just may be the first step.

Many blessings,

Mark Anthony
THE PSYCHIC LAWYER®

1

Spiritual Situational Awareness

Geronimo, the great Native American warrior, said, "We are all the children of one God. The sun, the darkness, the winds are all listening to what we have to say."

But are *we* listening to God?

God always pays attention to us. Unfortunately, we do not always pay attention to God. The messages transmitted by

God and from the Other Side are all around us—that is, if we are listening.

Situational awareness is the perception of what is happening around you in all directions at any given moment. This perception provides guidance for what course of action to take next. Situational awareness is a skill that is highly valued by police officers, firefighters, paramedics, and members of the military because it provides the ability to make snap judgments, which save lives.

Spiritual situational awareness is the perception of what is happening around you spiritually. It involves being open to contact from spirits. Spiritual situational awareness is highly beneficial because it can alter the course of your life. The challenge is recognizing the contact, accepting its reality, and then trusting its guidance.

I am lucky that my parents taught me about spiritual situational awareness. Both of them had psychic abilities and could perceive spirits. From a young age, I was trained to pay attention to the seen and unseen worlds around me.

I have been blessed by their lessons in many ways. As an attorney, I understand the value of paying attention to details; an attorney who doesn't is one who loses cases. As a medium, my parents' wisdom taught me that spirit contact and intuition are gifts from God that must be revered and respected.

IN MAY 2001, I arrived in New York City with my niece and nephew for a family reunion. I decided to take them on a tour of the city the day before the event. It was a bright and sunny Tuesday morning. The three of us took a cab to lower Manhattan to visit our cousin Reed, who worked in the South Tower of the World Trade Center. Reed met us in the plaza outside the Twin Towers.

"Here you are! At the center of the universe!" Reed exclaimed. He was excited about our visit and wanted to show us the incredible view from his office. At that moment, the World Trade Center appeared to be full of vitality, with thousands of people bustling about in every direction. However, my teenaged niece and nephew were more interested in shopping for clothes than in visiting the world financial center.

As I looked up at the spectacular Twin Towers glistening in the sun against a clear blue sky, I had a sudden feeling of dread—and then it happened.

A flash exploded in my mind's eye. Fear and helplessness flooded my entire body. I saw an inferno of fire and smoke with enormous chunks of debris plummeting downward toward me. Consumed by a horrifying fear that I was plunging to my death, my knees began to buckle. I felt like vomiting. Covering my face with my hands, I hunched over to brace myself. "Oh my god!" I cried out loud.

My niece and nephew stopped to stare at me, their mouths open.

"Dude—what is your problem?" Reed asked anxiously.

"I—I don't know," I stammered. "I saw something—something falling."

Within seconds the vision subsided. I looked up again at the Twin Towers, only to see them gleaming magnificently skyward.

"You know, Reed, if something should happen when you're up there in that building, you are trapped. I'm sorry, but I can't go up there."

Reed started to express his disappointment. My nephew eyed the Twin Towers suspiciously.

"Leave Uncle Mark alone," my niece interjected. "You know how he is."

I felt comfort in my niece's diplomatic and sensitive understanding of my psychic abilities. "Thanks," I whispered gratefully.

The mood of the moment lifted, and we told Reed we'd see him later at the reunion. My niece, who also never misses an opportunity to shop, quickly changed the subject. "Hey, look! A designer outlet store! Uncle Mark, would you please take us shopping there?"

I saw Gucci in her eyes—and I was more than happy to indulge the two of them. We quickly headed away from the Twin Towers.

Four months later, on September 11, 2001, I was at my law firm in Florida preparing for a court appearance. Suddenly, one of the other attorneys flung open the door to my office and abruptly entered.

"Something insane has happened! The World Trade Center in New York is on fire!"

"*What?*"

"Two jets just crashed into it! Both towers are burning! It's all over the news!" he exclaimed.

"Good Lord!" I breathed. It was all I could muster, remembering in horror what I'd seen four months earlier at the site. *My God—my cousin Reed!*

Frantically, I tried to call Reed, but to no avail. I called his wife, his mother, and his sister. No one could get through to New York City; all phone lines were jammed. Two days later, I was finally able to get through; Reed was alive.

Nearly a year later, Reed visited Florida with his wife and children. He took an afternoon to come and see me at my law firm.

Although he had survived the terrorist attack, I hadn't heard exactly what had happened to him. I'd heard from his wife that he had been in therapy for post-traumatic stress disorder. As he sat across the desk from me in my office, I could see he was clearly a changed man. Despite his smile, I saw deep wells of sadness in his eyes.

"I…I wanted to talk to you—about September 11," Reed said. "Somehow, I know you'll understand."

"What happened?" I leaned forward.

"It was about a quarter to nine in the morning, and I was in my office. I heard this sound like nothing I'd ever heard before—it had to be an explosion. I felt the whole office rattle."

Reed's facial features tightened. Articulating his experience had to be overwhelming for him.

"I left my desk and ran out into the hall. One of the secretaries screamed, 'A jet just flew into the North Tower—it's on fire!'"

I listened as Reed continued.

"I couldn't believe it! We all stood there watching from an office window. It was horrifying. The fire was spreading—smoke billowing, chunks of the North Tower flying everywhere. We were paralyzed with fear, not knowing what to do.

"My manager was on the phone with security. They told him that the Port Authority said everything should be okay, but if anyone wanted to leave, they should."

Reed paused and then said, "It was like that movie *Titanic*—you know, when the ship hits the iceberg and passengers are told everything is going to be okay, and somehow you know it isn't going to be okay. I thought about staying, but—but, well, I heard something weird," Reed explained.

"Weird? In what way?" I asked.

"For a second, I heard—in my head I heard—my grandpa Theorin's voice, and he said 'Go! Now!'"

"You and Theorin were very close, weren't you?" I regretted never having met my great uncle Theorin, who had died over a decade earlier. In a way I felt I knew him, since my father had told me a lot of colorful stories about him.

Reed paused. "Doesn't that sound weird to you?" My expression made Reed smile. "Oh yeah—*you* see dead people! Supposedly Grandpa Theorin could see them too."

"You know this ability runs in our family, Reed. So what happened next?"

"Well—I mean, seriously—who was going to get any work done with that going on?" Reed asked rhetorically. "I was freaked out enough from the plane crash, and then I heard a ghost! I knew I had to leave."

"Okay, what then?" I asked as Reed drew a deep breath.

"It was surreal. Everyone panicked," he described. "I was the last one into the elevator—sandwiched up against the doors."

"Why in the world did you take the elevator?"

"Supposedly, we had the fastest elevators in the world! I wanted to get out of there fast," he replied, pausing before continuing. "The elevator went down a few floors and—then—then—it started shaking all over the place. People were screaming; we were getting bounced around like crazy inside the elevator." He clenched the arms of his chair.

"Was that when the second jet hit the South Tower?" I asked.

"Yeah. The doors opened, and—I know this is going to sound crazy, but—" Reed hesitated.

"Go on, Reed, it's okay," I reassured him.

"When the elevator doors opened, I swear for an instant, like out of my peripheral vision, I actually saw Grandpa Theorin," Reed described. "He motioned to me. I knew I had to get out of the elevator, so I jumped out and fell on the floor. My secretary, Karen, and two other women fell next to me. The rest of the people were still in the elevator."

Reed continued. "I was lying flat on my belly next to these women. I turned and yelled to everyone, 'C'mon—get out!' But they didn't! They just stared at me…"

"What happened next?" My heart was racing.

"I looked back over my shoulder and—I…" Reed tensed before answering. "There was this sound—like another explosion—and the elevator burst into flames! Oh, Mark! I could see the eyes of some of the people who were still in it! My secretary…oh, my God, she just screamed—and the elevator—it was engulfed in fire! I saw the cables that hold the elevator snap—and it fell! Everyone was screaming. It was a giant ball of fire as it fell!"

Reed's whole body shook. With a trembling hand, I offered him a tissue.

"Burning embers were all over us. Karen and I rolled on the floor to put them out—it was horrible! The whole thing lasted only a few seconds…" Reed took a deep breath.

I tried to remain a calm and objective listener, but my heart was breaking for my cousin. My skills as a lawyer were being put to the test.

"Then—please don't think I'm nuts, Mark—I hear what sounds like Grandpa Theorin again. Now he says, '*Get up!*'"

"You're not nuts, Reed—please go on." I was on the edge of my seat.

"I got up and helped Karen and these two other ladies—I don't even know who they were—and we ran to the stairs…I must've been in shock! I felt my body going through the motions—it was like I was there but not there. The stairs were packed with people. The strange thing was, even though we were all in a state of panic, no one was shoving or pushing."

"And people say New Yorkers are rude," I said, trying to use some humor to diffuse the tension.

"I got to the lobby. It was unbelievable. The arched windows were shattered, marble walls cracked, elevators had crashed, artwork and statues were smashed. It was horrible," he continued.

"Finally I got outside." Reed paused. "Everything was out of control! People were running and screaming; firemen and cops were all over the place. Karen got separated from me in the crowd—she just disappeared. And then I heard—" Reed stopped and drew a deep breath.

"What did you hear, Reed?"

"I started to run to the right, but I saw—I mean, I felt—pulled to the left, and just for an instant I saw Grandpa Theorin, so I turned to the left, and as I moved, something hit the ground right next to me. I mean it missed me by a few feet—and it splattered all over me—and oh, the sound it made when it hit the ground! A *thud*," Reed said, tears streaming from his eyes.

"What almost hit you, Reed? What did you hear?" I asked in rapid succession.

"I heard a *thud*," he said, trembling.

"A thud?" I responded, not fully comprehending what he meant.

"A *thud*, Mark! A thud!" he repeated. "It was a body hitting the ground! It was a man's body—he hit the ground just feet from me! Stuff splattered all over me!" Reed began to sob. "Every time I close my eyes and try to sleep, I hear that sound...that *thud*."

I felt tears in my eyes.

"If it hadn't been for Grandpa Theorin, he would've landed on top of me!" he sobbed.

Horrified, I recalled the images from television of those who were trapped above where the jets hit the Twin Towers. Many jumped to their deaths rather than be burned up in the fire. Reed's experience made this all too real.

"I panicked. I thought I was going to puke!" Reed exclaimed.

The details of my premonition became hauntingly familiar.

"I ran and got caught up in the crowd. I fell and started getting trampled. I thought 'now I'm going to die,'" Reed recalled. He shook, struggling to maintain self-control.

"But then, I heard him again: Grandpa Theorin shouting but not shouting—it was in my head—and he said, 'Get up, boy! You gotta live!'"

I listened, transfixed.

"But I couldn't get up! People were stepping on me—trampling me," Reed described, fighting tears.

"Then this fireman—this young Latino guy—pulled me to my feet and asked if I was okay. I saw such fear in his eyes," Reed said, his own eyes closed.

"He rescued you," I suggested gently.

"Yeah, he did, and I don't even know how he saw me in the crowd. I've never respected anyone more in my life. Not because he saved me, but because this guy was scared to death too, and he was doing his job—caring more about other people than his own life."

We sat in silence as Reed regained his composure.

"Mark, you have to believe me. If it weren't for my grandfather's spirit, I wouldn't be here. It's like he reached out from heaven, telling me to leave, to get out of the elevator, which direction to run—I even think he sent that young fireman to save me. I'm so grateful—but, at the same time, so full of guilt that I'm alive."

"Survivor guilt?"

"That's what my shrink says, Mark."

Reed's hands shook as he reached into his pocket and pulled out a pack of cigarettes and a lighter. I'd never known him to smoke before.

"Uh, the law firm doesn't allow smoking in the office," I said hesitantly.

"I need it to calm my nerves," Reed responded, lighting a cigarette.

"You shouldn't smoke, Reed—it isn't good for you."

"Oh—like *it's* going to kill me?" he asked through a cloud of smoke.

"Well, it's a bad habit," I offered lamely.

Reed took a puff, smiled slightly, and retorted, "Smoking doesn't send you to hell—it just makes you smell like you've been there."

His slight smiled faded. "And I've been there."

THE MAGNITUDE OF spirit contact is immense. Contact from the Other Side is beneficial in many ways. For Reed, spiritual situational awareness saved his life. For my friend Emma, this awareness brought her peace and clarity at the end of her life.

Emma was an elderly woman living in South Africa. She heard about my work as a medium and my views on the everlasting nature of life during an interview on a worldwide radio broadcast. This prompted her to send me an email.

I opened her email and something—or, rather, some*one* in spirit—gave me the impression I needed to speak with her. I answered, indicating I'd welcome the opportunity to talk to her. The next day I received another email with instructions on how and when to contact her on a face-to-face Internet link.

When the link was established and her image appeared on the screen, I was stunned. Emma was lying in a hospital bed, propped up so she could see the computer screen and talk to the camera. She appeared extremely thin and very frail. I was surprised someone so ill had gone to such lengths to arrange a session with me.

A young South African man in a crisp white medical uniform stood next to her. "I'll be over here, ma'am, if you need anything," he told Emma before stepping out of the computer camera's view.

"This computer thing—it's really quite amazing, isn't it?" She smiled into the camera.

"Yes—yes, it certainly is," I responded.

"I've got cancer. They tell me I haven't long to live." Emma's blue eyes sparkled as if in defiance of the cancer that was consuming her. "I'm very much at peace about going home. I've never feared death. I feel a sense of completion and that it is just my time."

I was humbled by her courage in the face of impending death and wanted to help her in any way I could. Although I know that death is merely a transition, it is still frightening to most people. Yet somehow this Emma—this ray of light—seemed so unafraid.

"I feel spirits are around me. If you can, Mark, I would like to know who they are," Emma requested.

"Would you mind if we start our session with a prayer, as I believe prayer raises vibrational frequency?" I asked. When she nodded, I closed my eyes and prayed to God for guidance. Then I felt the connection with the Other Side.

When I had finished, I saw Emma gazing intently at me through the Internet link, so I began. "I see three women coming forward. Two are on the parent level, and one is on the grandparent level; all are connected to you through your mother's side of the family."

Emma listened quietly.

"Their relationship to you is very close. They feel like a mother, an aunt, and a grandmother. Your mother, or the woman who feels like your mother, has very light-colored hair—white hair—and very bright blue eyes. I see tremendous warmth in those eyes," I described.

Emma nodded. "Please, go on."

"One of the things I sense about your mother is the expression in her hands. Her hands are so soft and warm. I feel her reaching out in gentleness and taking your hand in hers. She says you get your strength from her."

"Mother had such lovely hands—and yes, they were very warm and soft," Emma confirmed.

"Your aunt is a thin woman. She wore glasses, and her hair was more gray than white. She was a quiet person who internalized her feelings and never spoke out when she felt that she had been treated poorly. Her inner quiet made her strong, but it was also her weakness. She never allowed anyone to know how much she suffered emotionally. In many ways, she epitomizes the expression 'long suffering,'" I conveyed.

"Aunt Justine," Emma sighed. "Such an unhappy woman."

"Her message to you is that the Other Side is free of suffering, and all the pain you go through in the material world is but a gateway to a joyous life on the Other Side—at least it was for her. That is what she wanted me to tell you."

"What about my grandmother?" Emma asked.

"Your grandmother's energy is quite different. She seems to be describing herself as quite the taskmaster with her children."

Emma nodded and tried to say something, but she began to cough.

"Your grandmother was not cruel, but she was a stern disciplinarian. She wanted her daughters to have more than she had and pushed them to be the best they could. Her forceful personality dwarfed your aunt—but not your mother. Your mother knew how to get around her strong character."

"You've captured their personalities," Emma said, struggling to suppress another cough. "What messages do they have for me?"

"They act as a unit of three on the Other Side. They're at peace with one another, and it feels as if they've been nurses to you in your pain and suffering. All of them want you to be spared this 'cup of pain,' but they also know that your journey isn't about to end—rather, it is to begin anew. They want you to understand this, to always focus on the Light, and to never be afraid. From the peace they project, they are in the heaven dimension of the Other Side."

As Emma's coughing intensified, the male attendant came into the camera's view. He reached toward the computer keyboard and said gently, "That's enough for today, Miss Emma."

My computer screen went dark. A few days later, I received this email from Emma:

Hello dear Mark,

I know you are worried about me. Do stop; I've had a good life. I want to thank you for the reading. The information was very accurate. I am so grateful! Thank you! It is so comforting to know they will be there when I cross over and that they have been there helping me all along. Heaven sounds so lovely.

I think we learn much through suffering. It deepens us and makes us more compassionate to the suffering of others. Somehow, I feel I was meant to experience this cancer and that is okay.

I am feeling very tired lately but am getting things in order. I have a lot of heat in my body, which gets very intense at times, and this is very draining. I am trying to be strong and asking God and his angels to not let it be too long. I look forward to being out of my body and free.

God bless you!

Emma

We continued to email each other for a few months. As Emma's emails became shorter and shorter, they seemed like a metaphor for the life force draining from within her. Eventually the emails stopped altogether.

One morning, I was in my office and thought about contacting the nursing home. Since I was not a family member, I knew they would not divulge any information. It was at that moment that I felt the nearness of a gentle and loving presence. It was Emma; she had passed away and had gone to the Other Side. It made me sad to have lost someone I'd come to know as a friend, and at the same time I was happy because her suffering was at an end. I had been privileged to touch the heart of this brave woman who had approached her death with total clarity and serenity.

Spiritual situational awareness has many benefits. It can be quite intense or it may be very subtle—but it is always powerful. While the messages were very different for Reed and Emma, paying attention to the Other Side proved to be, for them, gifts from God.

2

Inheriting the Double-Edged Sword of Psychic Ability

Gifts from God come in many ways, and sometimes they appear in the form of inherited abilities. Science is only beginning to unlock the intricate nature of genetics. Many traits—such as health conditions, athletic prowess, and intelligence—appear to have a basis in heredity. While everyone has the same basic physiology, genetics account for the fact that each of us has different mental or physical capabilities.

Studies conducted at UCLA have indicated that the speed of the brain's ability to process information is influenced by the brain's axons. Think of axons as the circuitry, or wiring, of the brain. Because the makeup of axons is governed by genetics, heredity has a great deal to do with intelligence. If intelligence is inherited, then other brain functions, including psychic and mediumistic abilities, are hereditary as well.

My family presents a strong case for the hereditary nature of psychic and mediumistic abilities. It would take an entire book just to chronicle all of the psychic and mediumistic activity in my family. They provide the best examples I know of for the hereditary nature of traits.

Before diving into my family's psychic gene pool, it is important to understand the basic distinction between psychic and mediumistic abilities. The terms *psychic* and *medium* are often used interchangeably. This makes sense because both of these abilities refer to a person who is sensitive to frequencies.

Psychics are sensitive to the energy of a person, place, or thing. According to theoretical physics, time is timeless. Simply stated, clocks don't really measure time. They provide a unit of measurement we can understand based on the earth's rotation. Psychics align their brain-wave frequency with energy that transcends our concept of time. This could explain why legitimate psychics are able to perceive past, present, *and* future events.

Mediums, on the other hand, perceive the energy of spirits. Basically, both psychics and mediums are sensitive to frequency; they just tune in to different "stations." This can be compared to the difference between AM radio and FM radio. It appears that all mediums have psychic ability, but not all psychics have mediumistic ability. By analogy, this means that psychics receive AM signals and mediums receive both AM and FM signals. This doesn't mean one gift is superior to the other—just different.

Psychic and mediumistic abilities have existed in my family for centuries. These abilities run on both my mother's and my father's sides of the family. When both parents possess a recessive trait, it increases the likelihood that at least one of their children will inherit these abilities. In my family, that child happens to be me.

PSYCHIC ABILITY IN my mother's family can be traced back to my great-grandmother, Giovanna Costa, in the late nineteenth century. Records and recollections of events prior to that time are fragmentary, and while she was not the first psychic in the family, Giovanna certainly stands out because of the unique talent she exhibited.

Giovanna was born in Scilla, Italy, an ancient seaside village surrounded by tall mountains that plunged into the crystal-blue waters of the Mediterranean. Located at the "tip of the toe" of Italy's boot, it is the closest point to Sicily, which sits just across the Straits of Messina. Due to its strategic location, one army after another had garrisoned Scilla since before the time of the Caesars. When Giovanna was born, the ancient fortress overlooking the town, which once commanded the turbulent waters between Italy and Sicily, had crumbled into ruin.

Even though it maintained a picturesque beauty, Scilla had become an impoverished village. The men of the Costa family were fishermen, specializing in swordfish. Swordfish was a highly prized delicacy in the posh restaurants of Naples, Rome, Florence, and Milan. Due to its high value, the Costas themselves couldn't afford to eat the swordfish they caught.

Giovanna's unwavering faith in God began at a young age. It was rumored among the villagers that she received visions from the Holy Spirit. Her devotion and piety led some to believe she was destined to be a nun. However, economic necessity required Giovanna to work for her family, and there was never an idle moment in her hard life. Waking before dawn, she cooked, cleaned, and helped her father, Domenico; her mother, Concetta; and her brother, sister, and dozens of other relatives. She possessed a sharp mind for numbers and eventually learned to manage the family fishing business.

In this era of devout Catholicism and arranged marriages, young women were matched with suitable young men and, after several chaperoned meetings, were expected to marry. Although this tradition seems medieval by today's standards, this was the norm at the time.

Giovanna was matched to Nunzio Pontillo. Despite the arranged marriage, they loved each other intensely. He was a dashing, handsome, and hardworking young engineer. Giovanna was a beautiful and statuesque woman who towered over the other village women. Despite his education, Nunzio couldn't find work. Prior to 1900, he left Scilla for America. He planned to live with Giovanna's brother, Lorenzo, who had recently moved to New York City. He would get a job, earn enough money to bring Giovanna to America, and they would start a family. Giovanna was excited at the prospect of a better life in America.

Nunzio found a construction job at Brooklyn Union Gas in New York. Giovanna, waiting in Italy, missed him dearly. She loved receiving his letters filled with descriptions of the exciting new world and relished the day they'd be reunited in New York.

However, one night in 1902, Giovanna settled down to sleep after a typical day of hard work. Once in bed, her thoughts ran to Nunzio, and she felt his warm and loving presence next to her.

Nunzio? With no warning, the warm presence eroded into a sick feeling in the pit of her stomach.

Holy Mary, Mother of God—NO! "Nunzio!" she screamed.

Hearing her cry out, her family rushed into her small bedroom. They found Giovanna sitting up in bed, sweating profusely.

"Nunzio!" she cried again.

"He's in America—he's not here!" her mother told her.

"No! I feel him—he's here! He's here—his spirit is here!" Giovanna began to sob hysterically.

"Giovanna, you just had a dream—a bad dream!" Her father tried to console her.

"I wasn't sleeping! I know something's happened—something terrible!" She collapsed into Concetta's arms.

Her family knew about her gift of seeing spirits, and although they tried their best to comfort her, there was no consoling Giovanna that night.

For three days, Giovanna didn't speak a word. She silently prayed she was wrong. *Was it just a bad dream? How could it have been a dream when I wasn't sleeping?*

On the fourth day, she received a telegram from her brother, Lorenzo, in Brooklyn, informing her that Nunzio had been crushed to death in an industrial accident along with five other young men. A huge gas tank broke free of its restraints and fell on the six men.

The grief-stricken Giovanna set sail for America seeking justice. She arrived in New York and moved in with her brother. Engaging an attorney, Giovanna proceeded to sue Brooklyn Union Gas for the wrongful death of her husband. After a lengthy legal battle, she received a settlement. With the money, she started an Italian lemon ice and ice cream business.

Although the young widow became financially successful as an entrepreneur, Lorenzo insisted she remarry. He arranged for her to marry Roberto Senna, a widower with five children. Together, they had four more children: my grandmother Angelina, Antonio, Concetta, and Lorenzo.

Giovanna and Roberto worked well together and turned the lemon ice business into a financial success. She was also active in the Catholic Church and the local community. Her acts of kindness and charity became well known. When nuns from Italy arrived in Brooklyn, Giovanna would house them, free of charge, until they were assigned to a convent. In addition, she took on the added task of helping them adjust to America. She spent time with the younger nuns to reassure them, and she consulted with the older nuns on matters of faith and the business of running a household. In the New York Italian community, Giovanna was regarded with the respect usually reserved for the Mother Superior of a convent—a great honor.

In time, Giovanna became a midwife and was considered by many to be a healer. She always seemed to "know" things. People trusted Giovanna's insights.

One day, she learned of the death of a little girl, barely sixteen months old. Since she had delivered the child, Giovanna and her eleven-year-old daughter, Angelina, attended the wake to console the family. In traditional Italian style, the viewing was open casket in the main room of their humble home. They were too poor to afford a service at a funeral parlor.

Giovanna arrived to find the devastated young parents surrounded by grieving family, friends, and the local parish priest. Rosary in hand, Giovanna approached the tiny coffin to pay her respects. Angelina stood by her side.

As Giovanna stared at the child's body, she sensed something.

"Mama! What are you doing?" Angelina asked as Giovanna reached into the casket and lifted the child from it.

Gasps flooded the room.

"Stop this sacrilege!" the priest exclaimed.

Ignoring him, Giovanna patted the baby's back firmly.

"What are you doing to my baby?" cried the little girl's mother.

The onlookers were mortified as Giovanna pulled open her blouse and placed the child's mouth to her breast.

"Desecration!" cried the girl's young father, who moved to stop her.

"Stay where you are!" Giovanna ordered with an out-stretched arm, the rosary dangling from her right hand, the baby cradled in her left. Angelina hid behind her mother for protection.

The young father obeyed. A gentle suckling sound emerged from the child at Giovanna's breast.

"She's alive!" Giovanna exclaimed, holding the child in her arms. The child coughed gently and continued to suckle at Giovanna's breast.

The silence of awe fell upon the room.

"Her spirit was still in her body," Giovanna told the stunned group

"A miracle!" cried the baby's mother as she ran to Giovanna, tears of joy washing down her cheeks.

Gingerly, Giovanna placed the little girl in the loving arms of her mother. The young father enveloped his wife and daughter in his arms.

"Forgive me for doubting you, signora," the priest apologized.

The child had been in a coma. Whoever had declared the little girl dead obviously had no experience with comatose subjects and had come to the wrong conclusion. But Giovanna sensed life remained in the little girl. She had learned to trust her gift of second sight and had the courage to act on her intuitive feelings. Had Giovanna not been there, the family would have buried the little girl alive. It was also fortunate for this family that embalming was cost prohibitive.

Needless to say, Giovanna's reputation spread throughout the Italian community and beyond. People flocked to her to receive the benefit of her wisdom.

IT APPEARS THAT inherited psychic abilities are recessive traits, which means they can skip a generation. None of Giovanna's children, including my grandmother Angelina, displayed psychic or mediumistic abilities. However, the next generation was another story.

My mother, Jeannie Aurena, was an extremely gifted psychic medium. Born in Newark, New Jersey, on the eve of the Great Depression to Rocco and Angelina Aurena, she was delivered by midwife—her grandmother Giovanna.

From the beginning, life was not easy for Jeannie. She had been born with several health challenges: an enlarged and slightly rotated heart, a tendency toward convulsions, and diverticulitis, a painful gastrointestinal condition.

Jeannie was especially close to her father, Rocco, who spent a lot of time with her. Because he was a sensitive and spiritual man, Jeannie felt he was connected to God. When Jeannie was sick, it was Rocco who stayed by her bedside and nursed her back to health.

Despite her medical issues, Jeannie was physically beautiful, had an upbeat, outgoing, and humorous personality, and gained a reputation for being the life of the party. With an infectious laugh, she had a way of making everyone around her feel like a friend. Growing up in Newark during the Depression could be dangerous, and Jeannie learned to take care of herself. She never tolerated bullies and sent more than one "tough guy" home with a bloody nose for picking on a physically smaller or weaker child.

Jeannie stood out from the other two children in her family because she talked to people others could not see. Even at a young age, Jeannie had the ability to see spirits; when she was very young, she considered them playmates. As she grew older, she realized that her friends were not visible to others. However, when Jeannie talked about her spirit friends to her parents, she was told to ignore them. Since the recessive trait of psychic ability had skipped her parents' generation, it was to her grandmother Giovanna whom Jeannie turned to for advice.

Jeannie often found comfort in Giovanna, who was known to her grandchildren as Nana. When Jeannie told Nana about her spirit friends, Giovanna counseled her not to be afraid and to keep this to herself. "I understand, because I see them, too. We have the gift of second sight. You can tell me, but don't tell anyone else—not yet, anyway."

Jeannie was a talented artist who painted in both watercolors and oils. To earn money on the side, she painted flowers on shower curtains and patterns on men's silk ties while attending the college of art in Newark. At the age of eighteen, she presented herself in such a sophisticated manner that people thought she was at least twenty-five. Jeannie's reputation as an accomplished artist grew. Soon, an executive at the Disney studios approached her and offered her a position as an animator in Hollywood.

Unfortunately for Jeannie, her father declared, "Good Catholic girls do not go running off across the country like a *putana* (whore) without a husband. I forbid it!"

Since in those days a father's word was law, Jeannie focused her creative talents closer to home. She worked in advertising and the art department of Kresge's, a major department store in Newark. Jeannie also became a great ballroom dancer. With shapely Betty Grable legs, she was also invited to become a leg model for Kresge's.

Jeannie developed a keen eye for designer clothes, dressing in a fashionably cosmopolitan style. With her natural beauty, artistic flair, designer clothes, sense of humor, and special intuitive sense, Jeannie had a reputation as a very elegant woman. She carried these traits her entire life. Not long after the end of World War II, she caught the eye of a handsome young sailor at a USO dance. His name was Earl Jay Anthony.

MY FATHER, EARL Jay Anthony, was born in Carbondale, Pennsylvania. He was a natural athlete who excelled at all sports, particularly baseball and boxing. Earl was agile, quick on his feet, and courageous. He never backed down from a fight, a trait his father, Earl, admired—and one his mother, Isabel, did not.

The Anthony family had been in America for over two centuries and was financially secure even during the Great Depression, owning a farm, a factory, coal mines, and a trucking business. They were conservative white Anglo-Saxon Protestants and lived in a large house on Main Street in Carbondale. My great-grandfather was a Baptist minister and founded a church there.

Even with their social standing, each family member had to contribute. The father—my grandfather—managed the family business, and my grandmother Isabel taught school. Young Earl's jobs included caring for the animals and stoking the coal-fired furnace to keep the house warm during the winter. It was while performing one of his many chores that Earl discovered his mediumistic ability.

Psychic and mediumistic abilities may seem like a gift to many people, but for ten-year-old Earl it felt more like a curse. He had to descend into a dark basement to shovel coal from the bin to the furnace. The downward climb into this dank space was not something Earl liked to do, for while he was in the coal bin, a male spiritual entity would "talk" to him. As is typical for a medium, he heard the voice not via sound waves but in the form of thoughts in his mind. However, this voice was not the voice he heard when he thought. It was definitely someone else's voice—and Earl didn't like it.

The spirit only talked to Earl when he was in the coal bin and didn't communicate with him anywhere else. The young boy was afraid to tell anyone for fear he'd be laughed at—or worse. Even at this age, Earl possessed enough common sense to realize "hearing voices" might not be a good thing.

He endured his duty as best he could. Whenever the house grew cold, his sisters—particularly his sister Margery—noticed his reluctance to go into the cellar. His other sisters and his younger brother teased him for being a chicken and afraid of the dark. Margery, however, did not.

Earl decided he must refuse to be frightened by the spirit and confront this entity.

"Shut up and get the hell away from me, you son of a bitch!" Those words became Earl's mantra every time he entered the basement.

I can hear you was the usual reply. The angrier Earl got, the more the spirit seemed to laugh at him.

Earl knew he couldn't challenge a spirit to a fist fight. Since arguing seemed futile, he figured out how to block the spirit; he simply began to ignore him. Over time, the spirit's communication diminished as Earl learned to disregard any attempts entirely.

By age sixteen, Earl seemed like a typical teenager, outgoing and athletic. He went to church on Sundays, worked for the family, and did well in school. But on the inside he felt isolated and alone because no one seemed to understand his peculiar ability—or so he thought.

On Thursday afternoons, when the men of the house were away at work, Earl's mother, Isabel, his grandmother Grace, and his sister Margery invited their lady friends over to the house for tea and a game of bridge. They convened in the Victorian-style parlor hung with elaborate draperies, visiting on the red silk–cushioned sofa and its matching chairs. The large mahogany table where they had their tea rested on a great oriental rug that covered most of the dark wooden floors. This was the cover story, at least.

One Thursday during summer recess, Earl came home early from working at the trucking business. He noticed the large oak doors of the parlor closed as usual. He always wondered what the big deal was with these Thursday meetings, so he decided to eavesdrop. He peered through the keyhole of the massive door, and what he saw and heard proved quite enlightening.

The women were gathered around the oval-shaped table in the center of the room. His grandmother, his mother, and Margery sat on one side of the table. Five other women sat across from them. All of them sat upright in their chairs with their palms flat on the table and their eyes closed.

He heard Isabel, his mother, speaking in a somber tone of voice.

"I'm seeing a man's spirit—it's your husband," Isabel said solemnly to the woman sitting directly across from her. "He knows you miss him—and the answer is, yes."

Earl, shocked, retreated to the kitchen to help himself to a piece of chocolate cake and wonder about what he had seen in the parlor. After the ladies left, he confronted his mother.

"Mom, what was that all about?" Earl asked.

"Oh! We heard a noise and thought it might be you," Isabel revealed.

"So, what were you doing?"

"Son, we were communicating with the Other Side," Isabel said nonchalantly.

"The Other Side of what?" Earl was confused.

"It was a séance, Earl!" his sister Margery interjected.

"Earl, it's important that you keep this secret!" Grandmother Grace interrupted Margery. "Your father and others in the family might not understand. The gift of spirit communication runs in our family."

"Yes, honey, we use our gifts to help people," his mother explained. "People need to understand that when someone dies, it isn't the end. They come to us and we help them."

"Help them? How? You can talk to spirits?"

"Yes, we can—and we can hear them, too," Isabel replied.

"Holy cow! So I'm *not* crazy!" Earl exclaimed.

"What do you mean? Is there something you need to tell us, dear?" Isabel turned to her son in surprise.

AT THE OUTSET of World War II, Earl joined the US Navy. After basic training, Earl was stationed aboard a Landing Ship Medium (LSM). The LSM ships were smaller vessels that brought landing craft and amphibious vehicles within range of the shore, enabling the marines to storm the beaches. Earl's ship was LSM 72.

Another facet of Earl's unusual ability emerged while he was in the navy. Just before going into battle, Earl noticed that when he looked at the other men on his ship, some of the sailors and marines appeared to have a strange gray and black veil over their faces and around their heads. Initially, Earl thought something was wrong with his eyes.

Why do only some of the guys have this creepy thing all over them? he wondered, trying to understand what he was seeing. However, after he'd survived several battles, a terrifying realization dawned on him. Whenever he saw this veil, the man died soon after.

Horrified, Earl realized he could foresee which people were going to die—and when they were going to die. The closer it came to the soldier's time of death, the darker and more pronounced the veil became. Just as he had done with the voice in the cellar, Earl kept this to himself. He feared he would be considered insane if he uttered a word to anyone. Worse, he didn't know what these sailors and marines would do to him if they somehow thought he was responsible for their doom.

What he was seeing was an aura. An aura may be best described as the energy field or radiating light that surrounds a person. Each human being has an energy field. This field radiates different vibrations and different colors, which some individuals are able to see. An aura often changes color depending on what is happening with that person emotionally or physically. The color of an aura can often be used to interpret the mood or health of an individual. Auras are often quite colorful, and some can be beautiful. But the auras that Earl Anthony saw were not vibrant, pretty colors. His ability signaled something much more ominous. The auras that he saw were dark gray and black. He knew when people were about to die.

Sadly, one day he saw most of the marines his ship was transporting into battle with this aura. It sickened Earl to see so many of his friends with the sign of death. He prayed that he would be wrong—that this whole matter was just a problem with his eyes. Unfortunately, the US Marines sustained a 90 percent casualty rate in that battle. That terrified Earl. He wanted desperately for what he perceived as a curse to go away. He did his best to ignore it, but he continued to see the aura of death anyway.

My father never mentioned this to anyone until much later, but this ability haunted him through the years. Later, when he did talk about it, he said, "No matter what, even though I could see it, there was nothing I could do to change the outcome for someone who was going to die. I couldn't even save my own mother."

Not long after Earl returned home from World War II, his mother, Isabel, was teaching a class. She had a sharp pain in her head, sat quietly at her desk, put her head down, and died. She was in her early fifties and succumbed to a brain hemorrhage.

Shortly thereafter, the family businesses went bankrupt as a result of his father's declining health and unwise business decisions. Although they were able to keep the family house on Main Street in Carbondale and the lake house in the country, everything else had to be sold.

My father found work at a factory in Newark, New Jersey, which was booming in the post-war economy. Not long afterward, he went to a USO dance and spotted, as he later described, a foxy woman named Jeannie. They fell in love and married after a four-year courtship. Earl had to convert to Catholicism, which wasn't well received by his Baptist family. While both Jeannie and Earl were people of faith, they realized that God and the afterlife went far beyond their respective religions. They were happily married for fifty-seven years.

WHILE IT IS wonderful to possess psychic abilities, it can also be a double-edged sword. When people around you possess them, too, it makes for a colorful and interesting life. What is it like when both your mom *and* dad are psychic? Most parents have some psychic connection with their children. In many instances it may be parental instinct, but in my family it was much more.

One rainy afternoon when I was nine, my fifteen-year-old brother, Earl Joseph, waited for three friends to come pick him up. One of his friends had recently obtained his driver's license and permission to drive his parents' car. This friend called and said he and two other teenaged boys were on their way to our house.

At the time, we had only one telephone in the house, and it was in the kitchen. As Earl Joseph hung up the phone, I noticed that my mother looked pale.

"Are you okay, Mom?" my brother asked.

"No, I'm not," she replied firmly. "I have a bad feeling about you going in the car with these boys."

"C'mon, Mom! We're just gonna go to the inlet and check the waves. It's raining—what can happen?" my brother, the surfer, rejoined.

"I have a bad feeling, Earl Joseph, and I don't want you to go," I heard Mom say.

"Jeez—gimme a break!" Earl Joseph begged.

"I don't want you going with these boys! You need to stay home!"

"For God's sake, Mom!"

"Please don't use language like that, Earl Joseph!"

"I want to go with my friends!" Earl Joseph insisted.

A sudden knocking on the door interrupted the escalating argument. Reluctantly, I answered the door and was relieved to see Patty, a neighbor girl who went to school with my brother. It had begun to drizzle outside, and despite her yellow raincoat, Patty looked a bit soggy.

"Hey, Earl Joseph! Do you want to go over to Mary's house with me and listen to some records?" Patty asked cheerfully.

Before my brother could even begin to respond, Mom grabbed her purse from the sofa and pulled a twenty-dollar bill from it—a princely sum for a teenager at the time.

"Earl Joseph, put on your raincoat," she said, practically throwing the twenty at him. "And here's some money for ice cream, too!" Mom exclaimed as she thrust the money into my brother's hand.

This prospect looked like a reasonable alternative to my brother. I could see he was mulling it over. Before he could mention his previous plans, Mom said, "Patty, Earl Joseph will be happy to go with you. The ice cream is on me."

Earl Joseph hesitated.

"Go with Patty—right now!" Mom practically pushed Earl Joseph and Patty out the front door into the drizzling rain.

Ten minutes later, a large white Buick screeched to a halt in our driveway. The drizzle had become a light shower. My mother and I went out to greet my brother's friends.

"Earl Joseph had to leave. He went somewhere with Patty. I'm sure he'll catch up with you boys tomorrow," she told the driver, who rolled down his window just enough to speak with us. By now, it was raining heavily.

"Bummer! We wanted him to hang out with us, Mrs. Anthony. Okay, tell him we'll see him tomorrow." They began to back out of the driveway.

"Boys!" Mom, standing in the soaking rain, called after them.

"Yeah?" the young driver responded. The rain had turned into a downpour.

"Boys, please—*please* be careful and drive safely today. Don't take any chances—don't speed!"

Barely acknowledging her, the driver put the car in reverse and, once on the wet street, sped away. Drenched, Mom and I went back inside the house. It was then that I noticed Mom holding the sides of her stomach and wincing in pain.

"Something bad—very bad—is going to happen." Her dark eyes fixed on mine.

Unfortunately, the young men chose not to heed her warning. Twenty minutes later, traveling at ninety miles an hour, the driver lost control of the vehicle and crashed into a telephone pole. All three boys were killed on impact.

News of the horrible tragedy spread rapidly through our small seaside community.

When my mother heard this, she went to her room and shut the door. I heard her weeping and then praying, asking God why those boys didn't listen to her. She also thanked God that her son had not been in that car.

My brother was shocked and couldn't believe his three friends had died. If it hadn't been for Mom's warning and Patty's surprise appearance, Earl Joseph would have been with them.

Later that evening, I overheard my parents talking in their bedroom.

"That could've been our boy in that car," Mom said.

"But he wasn't! Thank God you trusted your feelings, Jeannie," I heard my father say.

"Why didn't they listen to me?" Mom asked.

"I wish I knew, but Jeannie, this wasn't your fault. We can't make people listen," Dad consoled.

"Those poor boys! I can't imagine what their families must be going through." I could hear Mom weeping.

"Jeannie, I love you," my dad said.

Later that evening, my father sat down with both my brother and me to try to comfort us. He explained that no one is immune from tragedy. I'll never forget how he ended the conversation. "When your mother has one of her feelings—you listen to her!"

TEN YEARS LATER, when I attended college and joined a fraternity, a group of my fraternity brothers decided to spend the weekend at the beach. Since my parents' house was a block from the beach, we planned to camp in their backyard. About twenty guys between the ages of nineteen and twenty-three showed up at my house. Most had heard stories about my mother and her psychic abilities.

The weekend was filled with swimming and grilling hamburgers for this rowdy group of young men and the girls we'd met at the beach. Although some of my fraternity brothers were skeptical, a number of them asked my mother to give them a reading. To entice her, they hummed the *I Dream of Jeannie* TV show theme song in unison. Mom couldn't refuse their beguiling request. My friends were looking at the experience as entertainment—until Mom gave them a real show! She described some item or event in the life of each one of them with stunning accuracy. I laughed to myself at the looks of amazement on their faces. Laughter soon gave way to awe as Mom told them secrets about which she could not have known.

One particularly conceited fraternity brother insisted upon a personal reading. I noticed how she took his hand and held it. She hesitated before telling him, "You will have an easy life." He seemed pleasantly surprised and pleased with himself, as usual, and began to brag to everyone that Mrs. Anthony, the psychic, predicted he was going to have a lifetime of ease.

Later, I asked Mom, "Why did you tell that conceited jerk such a thing?"

She smiled. "I was being tactful. He's a big nothing. He will amount to nothing. There will be no real accomplishment of goals in his life. Basically, he's a shallow, self-centered fellow, so I said he'd have an easy life. What else can you tell a lazy person who happens to be a parasite and uses other people?"

Several years after college, I crossed paths with this man and, true to form, Mom had been right.

Sometimes the truth is painful because it isn't what a person really wants to hear. It is considered proper etiquette for a psychic to be tactful when being truthful, especially when the truth may be unpleasant. A person receiving a reading will be more receptive if information is presented in a diplomatic manner.

IN OCTOBER OF 1980, my father and my mother visited Las Vegas, Nevada. The newest addition to the Strip was the luxurious MGM Grand Hotel. Earl was eager to take Jeannie there.

As they walked into the lobby, Earl marveled at the opulence of the MGM Grand. "Jeannie, isn't this place great?"

Jeannie found herself feeling something very different. For her, the lavishness of the MGM Grand quickly turned into a terrifying experience.

"Earl, I feel dizzy and hot," Jeannie murmured.

"Are you sure it's not menopause?" Earl joked.

"It's not a hot flash!" Jeannie glared angrily at Earl.

"What's going on with you, Jeannie? Are you okay? My goodness, you're shaking!"

"I'm dizzy—and hot! It feels like heat from a fire! I—I can't breathe!" Jeannie gasped, perspiring profusely as a rising terror began to grow within her. Unsteady on her feet, she collapsed into Earl's arms.

Hyperventilating, she managed to say, "Earl! It's a tomb!"

"What?"

"It's a *tomb*! Oh my god, get me out of here! *It's a tomb!*" she cried.

"Okay, okay! Hold on, Jeannie," Earl whispered, helping her toward the entrance of the hotel.

"I see death! I can't breathe! Oh my god, get me out of here!"

Panic-stricken with the realization that this was a premonition of a terrible event to come, Jeannie repeated, "It's a tomb! It's a tomb!"

After decades of marriage, Earl knew when Jeannie was having a premonition and quickly got her outside in the open air. As soon as they left, her physical symptoms subsided. Still, she felt completely drained and refused to return to that hotel under any circumstances. The mere mention of the place made her shudder. When my parents returned home, I remember my mother telling me about her feelings at the MGM Grand Hotel.

The following month, on November 21, 1980, wiring connected to a refrigeration unit sparked a terrible fire in the MGM Grand. It spread rapidly, engulfing everything—including wallpaper, glue, PVC piping, and other plastic materials. Lethal toxic fumes were produced and sucked into the air-conditioning distribution system, spreading poisonous gases and black smoke throughout the building. Nearly 5,000 people were in the complex when this occurred. Casualties were heavy: 84 people killed and 784 injured.

Toxic smoke inhalation caused most of the deaths. Many of the victims were trapped in stairwells as they were trying to escape. Firefighters found five of the dead holding hands. Just after she pressed the emergency call button on the elevator, a woman was overcome by the toxic smoke and fell to the ground. Her finger left a trail through the soot on the wall from the elevator call button to the floor.

The shining new gem of the Las Vegas Strip became what Jeannie had foreseen: a tomb.

INHERITING BOTH PSYCHIC and mediumistic abilities is a double-edged sword. People who do not understand them often conclude they are somehow negative. This has resulted in centuries of tremendous discrimination and persecution against people with these abilities.

My father's sister, Margery, was a psychic medium. She inherited a highly developed precognitive ability, which meant that she had the ability to sense things before they occurred. Like the other psychics on my father's side of the family, she seldom spoke of her abilities to people outside of the family and those who sought her advice.

She married a man named Lyle, and they started a family. Margery was an exceptionally intelligent woman who was very emotionally sensitive. Although she was not religious per se, she believed deeply in God and was very spiritual. Lyle, on the other hand, was extremely religious and did not appreciate his wife's psychic abilities. He believed it was the work of the devil to foresee the future and, even worse, to speak to the dead.

After flunking out of medical school, Lyle found work as a machinist at Crucible Steel in Harrison, New Jersey. One morning, when he was getting ready for work, Margery insisted he not go that day. He tried to shrug off her concerns, but she became adamant.

"Lyle, I'm afraid for you—please don't go to work today."

Lyle responded angrily. "Would you stop it?"

"Lyle! You *cannot* go to work today!" Margery demanded.

"Did one of your boogiemen tell you something?" Lyle sneered sarcastically.

"I love you, and if you go to work today, I'll never speak to you again!" Margery retaliated. Lyle was stunned. Margery was normally reserved and soft spoken. He finally relented and did not go to work.

That very day, a crane was maneuvering tons of steel beams over the machine shop where Lyle worked. A cable snapped and the steel plummeted to the ground, crushing his workstation and killing all of his coworkers.

Margery's premonition, her intuitive precognitive ability, saved his life. However, when Lyle heard about this, he was furious with Margery.

"You do the work of the devil! *You* did this!" he accused.

"Lyle! How could you say such a thing?" Margery cried, close to tears.

Because of his fundamentalist religious beliefs, Lyle rejected any notion that Margery's abilities were a gift from God; he saw them as evil. Lyle's attitude toward Margery and her psychic abilities caused her tremendous anxiety. She pleaded with him to understand. Patronizing her, he said, "Never mind. Everything will be fine, dear. Maybe we both need to take some time off and go to the lake for a vacation."

Two weeks later, the entire family gathered at the lake house in the mountains of Pennsylvania. My parents, Earl and Jeannie, were among the family members invited. They brought my sister, just a toddler, and my infant brother.

The lake house, a large two-story home in rural Pennsylvania surrounded by hills and forests, was the perfect place for a family reunion. Late one evening, after the children were asleep and the adults were getting ready for bed, Lyle asked Margery to stay downstairs with him.

She said, "I'm really ready to go upstairs to bed, Lyle. Why don't we retire for the night like everyone else?"

At that moment, there was an abrupt knock on the front door. Lyle asked Margery to please get up to see who would visit at this late hour. Two men in white uniforms from the state mental hospital stood waiting outside. They asked for Margery.

Margery backed away from the front door, her eyes filled with terror.

"Who are these men, Lyle? What are they doing here?" she asked, her body trembling. She turned to run upstairs, but Lyle grabbed her by the arm and held her fast. The two men pushed into the house to take Margery from Lyle.

"Stop! What are you doing to me? Lyle! Stop them!" Margery called to Lyle for help as they tried to subdue her, shoving her thin arms into a white straightjacket.

"Lyle! For God's sake!" she shouted. "I'm not crazy! Tell them I'm not crazy! Didn't I save your life?" Desperately, she looked to Lyle for help.

As the men pulled her out of the house, they belted the leather straps across her back. Margery's shouts woke everyone upstairs, including the children. Her cries for help were searing. Awakened family members hurried from their beds to see what was happening. The children looked out the windows while some of the adults grabbed for their robes and stumbled down the grand staircase.

Watching in shock from the top of the stairs, Jeannie, with my sister sobbing in her arms, cried out, "Margery! Earl—do something!"

Earl shouted, "Lyle! What the hell are you doing?"

"I have my legal rights as her husband, Earl. Stay out of our business!" Lyle bellowed to his brother-in-law.

My father lunged down the stairs, but it was too late. The uniformed men already had Margery in the ambulance and were pulling out of the driveway. They could still hear Margery's pleas for help. My sister cried for Aunt Margery, who had always been so kind to her.

Jeannie turned to her husband. "We're leaving, Earl. I won't stay another night under this roof with that man," she said, pointing to Lyle in disgust.

Lyle retreated outside and into the dark night.

At the mental hospital, Margery was diagnosed with schizophrenia coupled with hallucinations, delusional ideation of foretelling future events, and seeing ghosts.

"I'm not insane. I know what I'm doing. Please, please believe me," Margery begged the doctors and nurses.

Fully restrained, staff aides strapped Margery to a gurney. Weeping, she braced herself when she felt the cold gel used to attach electrodes to both sides of the head for bilateral electroshock therapy, the accepted treatment for schizophrenia at the time.

Even though she was sedated in preparation for the electroshock therapy, Margery sobbed and cried out to Lyle to rescue her. She screamed for someone to understand. The screams continued until they applied the voltage. As the first wave of electricity surged through her, she convulsed. When the doctor applied another and then another surge of electricity into Margery's brain, her screams became muffled cries.

After several more treatments during her nearly six months in the mental hospital, Margery returned home. A somber mood greeted her when she entered her house.

Lyle tried to embrace the fragile and tired-looking Margery, but she rebuffed his affection. She meekly acknowledged her husband, slowly climbed the stairs to her bedroom, and closed the door behind her.

Margery was never the same. Once a high-strung, energetic, and articulate woman, she had become sullen, withdrawn, and forgetful. Margery never spoke of seeing spirits or of having premonitions again. She lived another twenty years and died as she had lived, quietly and with elegance.

MY FAMILY HISTORY illustrates that inheriting psychic and mediumistic abilities can be a double-edged sword. Throughout the ages, psychics and mediums have often been cursed instead of seen as possessing a gift. For some primitive reason, these abilities inspire fear in many people. In the medieval era, such seers were charged with witchcraft and burned at the stake. The prevalent belief was that prophecy and contact with spirits meant someone was in league with the devil. In more recent times, as in the case with my aunt Margery, these abilities have been categorized as mental illness. Even today, we are confronted by fear-driven religious fanatics and closed-minded people who believe all psychics and mediums are deranged or, at best, charlatans.

Even though I have endured insults and criticism from people who do not understand or believe in interdimensional communication, I am thankful that I live in a free country and in an era when these abilities can be discussed more openly. For me, my inherited ability is a blessing, not a curse. I am honored to be a descendent of such courageous ancestors, some of whom were venerated, others who were persecuted.

I was four years old when my ability to perceive spirits emerged. Mom took it in stride, but it greatly worried my father. Maybe it reminded him of his childhood, or perhaps it brought back darker memories—those of a sensitive and fragile woman pleading for mercy, abducted in the middle of the night because she had inherited a gift that allowed her to see the future and communicate with spirits.

Entering the
Veil of Heaven

The great scientific minds in physics, including Albert Einstein, Richard Feynman, and Stephen Hawking, have theorized that time is actually timeless. The idea is that everything that has happened, is happening, and will happen is occurring simultaneously—at least in the energetic sense. Our reality is that time exists because our perceptions are based on the finite. While in physical form, we are incapable of truly understanding infinity.

"What happens when we die?" is one of the most frequently asked questions, and for good reason. People fear the unknown—and death is certainly the great unknown for the vast majority of people. Faith in God helps sustain us through times of uncertainty. Faith is the cure for healing the fear of the unknown.

For some, belief is split into different camps, usually the faithful versus the scientific. My belief is that faith and science are not diametrically opposed. Albert Einstein once remarked, "Science without religion is lame; religion without science is blind."

During a reading I conducted for Gemma, the spirit of her best friend came through. Gemma was concerned that she'd never see her friend again because her friend had died ten years earlier. The spirit responded with this message: "Today is yesterday and tomorrow is the past as yesterday is the future. None of it matters, there is no time."

Spirits have often communicated to me that there is no time on the Other Side. Therefore, even though Gemma might live another fifty years after the death of her friend, by the spirit's reckoning, she'll be reunited with her in a few moments. Spirits don't cease to be able to communicate with those of us in the material world, no matter how long they've been on the Other Side. There is no shelf life for spirit contact. Certainly they're busy and evolving in the spiritual sense, yet they can always communicate with us.

It is natural for those of us in the material world, particularly in Western cultures, to think of time as linear. We are born, we grow old, and then we die. Our concept of time may be analogized to drawing a dot on a blackboard and then a line from left to right. The dot is our birth—what we believe to be our starting point. The line symbolizes our life—how we grow from childhood through adulthood. When the line stops at the right side of the board, this represents our physical death. Simple, right?

Science has given us a glimpse of what the Other Side is like. Survival of consciousness studies are a scientific effort to answer the question of what happens when we die. In the 1970s, the great Dr. Raymond Moody initiated an entire field of research into what is known as a near-death experience (NDE). Since then, numerous studies about people who died and were resuscitated have been conducted worldwide.

Dr. Kenneth Ring of the University of Connecticut, one of the foremost researchers in the field of near-death experiences, found significant similarities in what people encounter during an NDE. The subjects often describe their consciousness separating from the confines of the human body, followed by a feeling of floating and a sensation of well-being and peace. The subjects then recall traveling through a tunnel toward a great white Light filled with intelligence and love. When entering the Light, the subjects mention encountering spirits of people they know who have died. These spirits are there to greet and guide the person's entry. Dr. Ring has noted these similarities exist despite a person's gender, age, marital status, education, social class, ethnicity, religious affiliation, or cause of death.

According to Dr. Jeffrey Long, founder of the Near-Death Experience Research Foundation, the largest database of near-death experiences in the world, the conclusions of near-death experience studies is that consciousness survives physical death. In other words, who and what we are continues to exist independently of our physical body.

What is the Light? Based on my work as a medium and my work with mediums, spiritualists, scientists, and people of faith worldwide, I believe the Light represents a human's perception of what can only be described as the spiritual energy of God. God is the spiritual being, and we, as spiritual beings having a material world existence, were created in God's image. We are all "cells" in the infinite body of God. Perhaps Albert Einstein described it best: "Matter is Energy. Energy is Light. We are all Light Beings."

Since the dawn of recorded history, all the great religions have described God in terms of Light. The NDE studies support this description. People who have a near-death experience tend to describe the Light as just that—an encounter with God. This occurs even if that person had been an atheist prior to the NDE. Nancy Evans Bush, the president emeritus of the Near-Death Experience Society, has said, "Most near-death experience subjects say they don't think there is a God—they know there is a God."

Many scientists who initially questioned the existence of God and who conduct survival of consciousness/near-death experience studies conclude that an afterlife does exist. Evidence looks different to those who are skeptical and those who have closed minds. A skeptic questions and seeks proof; ergo, he or she is open to evidence that God and an afterlife exist. A person with a closed mind has already made a decision and will not change, much less consider evidence.

Evidence is crucial in my work as an attorney. When selecting a jury prior to a trial, I seek jurors who are open minded about a situation and who look forward to making a decision based on evidence rather than preconceived notions.

Near-death experience studies focus on people who were clinically dead yet returned to their bodies, living to tell the tale. What about those who did not return to the material world? In the thousands of readings I have conducted, many people ask, "Who greeted my loved one?" or "What was crossing into the Light like?"

Perhaps the best way to find out is to simply ask the residents of the Other Side.

TELEPHONE READINGS ARE just as accurate as readings in person, and they add an additional element of anonymity between the client and me. This means I do not know the age, ethnicity, socioeconomic status, or anything else about the client prior to the reading. During a telephone reading with Kate, the spirit of her mother came through.

"Your mother was very ill, Kate. I sense a tremendous amount of physical problems and complications," I described.

"I'm experiencing weakness and feeling very frail. Your mother says she knows you don't want to hear this; however, she was ready to go."

"She was ninety-two years old when she passed," Kate stated. "I know that's old—but it still hurts so much. We were very close. I'm curious, Mark. Can you tell me who was there to greet my mother? What was crossing into the Light like for her?" Kate asked.

Suddenly the energy from her mother's spirit intensified. The feelings of frailty she had transmitted to me were converted into a vigorous sensation. Literally, I felt energized. This was not what I would have expected from a ninety-two-year-old woman. However, I remembered we are not these bodies; we are temporarily housed in these bodies. She was no longer ninety-two years of age; she was now an immortal living spirit.

"Her death and separation from her body was a jolt," I explained to Kate. Many spirits have told me of the separation from their bodies, but Kate's mom went into extreme detail.

"A jolt?" Kate inquired.

"A jolt—like a shock. Like a minor electrical shock." The spirit of Kate's mother continued to transmit the explanation in a way I could explain.

"You know those little 9-volt batteries, the kind you put in an alarm clock to keep it running in case the electricity goes out?"

"Yes, I know what those are," Kate affirmed.

"It feels like when you put your tongue on the battery to see if it still holds a charge, and you get that shock—more like a tingling on your tongue, right?" I described.

"Yeah," Kate giggled. "I've actually done that."

"Well, that is what she says the jolt feels like. It's a small electrical type of shock that kind of tingles—and then she separated from her body. It didn't hurt. It was just a jolt."

"Can you tell me any more?" Kate sounded intrigued.

"For a few seconds your mom looked down at her body in the hospital bed, and then she turned away. She says she started to walk up a stairway—a very dark staircase," I conveyed.

"It was dark?" Kate whispered with alarm.

"Hold on—give me a moment…" I continued as the imagery from Kate's mom unfolded. "It looks like an old wooden staircase. She just took a few steps up and there was a door—a rough wooden door with black metal hinges…"

"I don't know if I want to hear this," Kate said, obviously frightened.

"Holy smokes!" I exclaimed.

"What?" Kate cried out.

"The door—it just flew open!"

"Keep going!" Kate pleaded.

"It's so bright!"

"What—what is so bright?" Kate asked, her excitement now palpable.

"The Light is such a bright white and blue—like a sky blue mixed in with pure white light. Now I can see the outlines of people. There are one, two, three—no, wait! Seven people are there!"

"Who are they?" Kate wanted to know.

"They're beginning to take form…this is so cool!" I was elated. "They're becoming recognizable. Okay, this is happening pretty fast! Let me see—I need to describe them to you."

"Tell me!" Kate exclaimed.

"The tallest, or at least the one closest, is a male. This man is tall and lean, more like a medium build. He has a receding hairline and is clean-shaven with a fair complexion, dark eyes, and a happy demeanor. He reached out to your mom. I feel this great sensation of love—he definitely knows and loves her. He said, 'Welcome aboard!' I get the impression he was a sailor or in the navy," I detailed.

"That's my grandfather! My mother's father! He was tall and had a receding hairline—and he was in the navy!" Kate cried.

"The woman next to him is a good head shorter than he is. She has beautiful silver-gray hair styled very nicely. She is well groomed and elegant," I explained.

"Gram! That's my grandmother! She always looked so smart and made sure she always had her hair done, right up to the time she passed!" Kate recounted.

"The feeling of love and peace is incredible," I described. "I'm trying to see if the others will step forward. They are close to your mother, but this is really intense. It is an ultra-high frequency—and hard to hold," I said, focusing as hard as I could.

"See if you can, please," Kate asked. "I'd like to know everything!'

"Your mother wants you to understand what her experience of crossing into the Light was like. She is taking me further into the Light. She is definitely surrounded by her parents and other people she loves. The feeling of love flowing through me is very, very strong!"

Kate listened intently.

"What?" I almost shouted in the phone. "They're telling me that this is as far as I can go," I said to Kate.

"C'mon guys, give me a try," I pleaded with the spirits, straining to maintain the intensity of the connection. I was giving this everything I had.

"It is not that we don't want to show you. It's just that, in the form you're in, you cannot understand what it is truly like," Kate's grandfather explained. "It is beyond your ability to perceive."

I conveyed this to Kate and described, "Your mother is turning to me and smiling. She is enveloped in love and the beautiful, bright Light. She loves you and says she'll see you in your dreams."

"I do dream about her!" Kate commented.

With that, the link with the Other Side vanished. I fell back in my seat, sweating from exhaustion and, at the same time, exhilarated beyond measure. Touching the energy of the heaven dimension of the Other Side had been amazing, intense, and extremely humbling.

"Why do you think you couldn't go further?" Kate asked.

I thought for a moment. "The best way I can describe it is that I'm operating like an old dial-up modem on a computer and their energetic functioning is faster than high-speed Internet. It's kind of like I'm a single wire trying to channel all the electricity flowing into New York City; I simply cannot process it. Humans aren't equipped to handle that much energy. It was awesome."

I HAVE HAD several experiences during readings where spirits have enabled me to feel what it was like for them to cross into the periphery of the Light and encounter loved ones already on the Other Side. It appears that a human's ability to perceive is extremely limited while in physical form. We may be able to briefly experience the periphery of the Other Side, the veil of heaven, but while we are still physically alive, we can go no further.

NDE subjects report a similar situation. They encounter loved ones in the Light and wish to go forward with them. They want to embrace the sensations of overwhelming love and peace they experienced in the Light, which are beyond description in physical terms.

However, the reason it is a *near*-death experience is that the NDE subject is halted at a certain point. As the vast majority of those who have experienced an NDE report, the welcoming spirits of loved ones tell them they must go back into the physical realm because it isn't their time yet. This transitory point is the entrance, or the beginning level, to the

Other Side. This is where the "decision" is made as to whether the subject returns to the material world or continues the transition into a state of pure spiritual energy.

Now the question becomes: what lies beyond the veil?

4

Levels of the
Other Side

O nce you enter the veil of heaven, then what? You and
I live in the material world, which is finite. Everything
we know has limits and boundaries, beginnings and ends.
Our perceptions are therefore determined and processed in a
constrained manner. Fully comprehending the Other Side is

beyond our capabilities since we are trying to understand the infinite from a finite perspective.

Yet, human beings are instilled with an insatiable curiosity. And the fact that we may not be capable of completely understanding the infinite nature of the Other Side does not stop us from trying. That is why the path to discovery and wisdom always begins with the statement "I don't know." However, it helps to focus on what we *do* know.

At any given moment we are surrounded by invisible waves of energy loaded with vast amounts of information. We may not be aware of this energy, but it's there. If you don't believe me, then simply switch on a radio.

You've probably listened to the radio thousands of times and know that it's not magic; it's technology. Science has shown us that energy cannot be created or destroyed; it can only be transferred from one form to another. Most forms of energy travel in waves such as light waves, sound waves, and radio waves.

Radio waves are a form of energy humans cannot perceive, despite our knowledge that it exists. Technology—meaning your radio—converts the energy of radio waves into the energy of sound waves, which the human ear can perceive. This now brings us to frequency and amplitude.

In physics, frequency is a means of measuring the rate at which something occurs during a given period of time, like radio waves. Amplitude is the measurement of the length and width of these waves as they occur or vibrate.

To simplify, think of jumping on a trampoline. The number of times you jump on a trampoline in one hour is your frequency. How high you jump is your amplitude.

With these basic definitions of frequency and amplitude, let's return to your radio. The radio bands and frequencies are numerous. When one overlaps another, it is known as radio frequency interference. That is why tuning in to a radio station of your choice sometimes requires effort. Other times it does not because the reception is clear for that station. All of these bands of radio waves are energy, and they account for an infinitesimal fraction of the unseen energy surrounding us.

When our physical body ceases to function, the energy that was temporarily housed in that form is released to what I refer to as the Other Side. Just as there are different bands of frequency to the energy known as radio waves, there are different bands of frequency on the Other Side. It is not just one stagnant state. The Other Side contains a multitude of frequencies that may be thought of as levels. This is something that people of faith have understood for a long time.

For the past 5,000 years, religions have taught that there are different dimensions, or levels, to the Other Side. Hindus and Buddhists believe the Other Side has many levels, although they may differ as to the number of these levels. The ancient Egyptians, as well as the Mediterranean religions of ancient Greece and Rome, portrayed the afterlife as having different levels. As an example, those who possessed valor were sent to paradise; those who committed acts of evil and treachery were sent to places of eternal punishment.

Although Judaism does not necessarily define the nature of an afterlife, traditional Judaism teaches that death is not the end of human existence. Judaism does refer to a higher state of being after physical death known as *olam ha-ba* ("the world to come").

Christianity has different levels, or dimensions, to the Other Side. Jesus said, "In my Father's house are many mansions" (John 14:2). Many scholars have interpreted this to mean that there are many dimensions to heaven.

Islam teaches there are different levels of heaven. The belief is that there is one hell and one paradise, although each of those has levels.

As a Catholic who seriously considered entering the clergy, I was raised to believe in yet another dimension to the Other Side, which is purgatory. In legal terms, one might think of purgatory as a form of cosmic probation. If you were not quite good enough to go to heaven and not bad enough to be condemned to hell, you went to purgatory, where your soul could atone for deeds done in life. The souls who go to purgatory stay there for a length of time and eventually ascend into the higher levels of heaven.

In discussing the views of various religions, it is neither my place nor my intent to pass judgment upon any belief system. As an attorney, I believe in freedom of religion. As a man of faith, I've traveled the world and met many people of different faiths. I've been fortunate to have discussions with Christian ministers, Catholic priests, Greek Orthodox priests, Jewish rabbis, Muslim imams, Hindu priests, Buddhists monks,

Native American shamans, Taoist ministers, and Spiritualist ministers. Each of them has been rewarding and insightful beyond measure. Once we get beyond our cultural differences and biases, we all have a profound belief in common: that of a loving God.

My experience has shown me that truly faithful people believe good is rooted in love and nonviolence. I've also seen that those who seek to use a religion to justify anger, bigotry, hatred, or violence are not acting according to the will of a loving God but in furtherance of their own self-centered, egoistic agendas.

WHILE IN FINITE form, we may not be able to completely grasp how these levels of the Other Side work and interact with each other. I've found it helpful to ask those who reside in infinity what it is like.

The reading I conducted for Zoey was quite challenging. As soon as I opened up spiritually to receive contact, a young boy came forward. He had an incredibly energetic spirit, and it took some doing to keep up with the rapid vibration of his ultra-high frequency.

"That's Jordan!" Zoey responded. "My little boy had so much energy!"

"It is hard keeping up with him, but he is so full of joy and happiness. He loves you very much. It looks like he didn't like to sit still for very long! I guess that isn't unusual for a young child, but he also had another attribute he is conveying. He could focus his attention intently on something if he chose. He used to listen to you and actually hang on your every word."

"He did," Zoey confirmed.

"Jordan also wants to acknowledge the photos—framed photos—you have of him on a dresser. There is also a votive candle. I believe it is a white votive placed near the photos. This is where you honor his memory."

"I have such a place in my home." Zoey's face softened.

"His death was sudden," I conveyed. "I'm experiencing a bitter taste in my mouth—almost metallic in nature. This is odd. I can't quite put my finger on it."

"I understand exactly what you are saying," Zoey said stoically.

"He is switching tracks now and wants to focus on happier things," I told her. "He liked basketball a lot. It's funny because he couldn't really dribble or shoot—it seems as if the basketball was too large for him to handle. But he would try and try, even though there was no way he could succeed."

"Jordan was only three years old, but he was obsessed with sports. Basketball was his favorite. Basketballs were too big for him, but he tried to play anyway; that's funny."

"Now he wants to talk about your husband." I sensed a change of subject.

Zoey paused. "Please, go on."

"There is some kind of separation between the two of you. I see your husband running around holding the sides of his head. It's like he has a horrible headache. He is screaming—screaming about something horrible."

"That makes sense; please tell me more." Zoey's voice became a whisper.

"There is a sharp pain in my left temple." I described the sensations transmitted by her husband's spirit. "And I am getting the impression your husband is left-handed."

"He was left-handed," she confirmed.

"This is confusing." I paused, trying to assimilate the rapid transmission of information from this spirit. "He seemed like such a kind and loving man, yet prone to rage."

Zoey listened intently.

"'What have I done? What have I done?' He keeps repeating this," I relayed.

"That makes perfect sense." She paused before adding, "Mark, I have to tell you something."

"Are you sure you want to do that? My policy is to have the client tell me very little." I wanted her to get the full benefit of the reading.

"No—I know how my husband, Kurtis, died. I'm more interested in what he and my children have to say," Zoey explained.

I listened as Zoey continued. "Kurtis was being treated for depression with medication. The doctor switched his medication, and he apparently had a bad reaction to it. Normally he was a loving and kind man—the darling of his family, the ideal husband and father, and then—"

"He completely lost control," I interjected. I felt forced to communicate that message from Kurtis's spirit. I dreaded what was coming next.

"One day he said he'd watch the kids—I told him I'd get some takeout for dinner." Zoey gasped for breath. I closed my eyes as the images projected from Kurtis appeared in my mind's eye. She continued, "When I got home, I found…he had…"

I felt tears well up in my eyes, knowing what was coming.

"He'd—he'd taken his gun—and shot my three-year-old son in the back of the head. That's why you tasted metal in my son's mouth. And then he ran outside and murdered my five-year-old daughter—and then he blew his own brains out." Zoey's shoulders slumped.

My experience as a lawyer has made me tough, yet nothing could have made me tough enough for this. Zoey's agony was beyond belief. However, as a professional, I knew I had to continue with the spirit connection.

"This explains," I continued, "why, prior to his death, he was running around holding his head and screaming, 'What have I done? What have I done?'" I paused for a moment. "Kurtis says that after he did this, it was as if a fog lifted. He understood what he'd done and was so horrified, he couldn't stomach it—and so he ended his own life," I told her.

"I'm surprised my daughter didn't come through," Zoey said with quiet disappointment.

As soon as the words left Zoey's lips, I perceived the presence of a beautiful young girl. I described her long dark hair and dark eyes—and gregarious personality.

"That is Jada," Zoey confirmed.

"Both of your children are with your husband. I see him on his knees with his hands folded in prayer. He was a handsome man! His large dark eyes are filled with a profound sadness. There are tears in his eyes. He begs your forgiveness."

"Does he?" Zoey asked.

"There's more," I conveyed. "Your children are standing on either side of him. They each have an arm around his shoulder. They are saying, 'We forgive you, Daddy.'"

Zoey sighed from exhaustion. "I'm trying to forgive him, I'm just not ready to—maybe I never will be, even though I understand how healing forgiveness can be," Zoey revealed. "In fact, I'm a grief counselor."

I sat in silence, knowing she needed to tell me more.

"While I understand the phases of grief one has to go through, this certainly has put me to the test. In one afternoon I lost my babies, my husband—my whole family. His family has been destroyed, too. He was the favorite son— his parents couldn't understand how Kurtis could do such a thing. Even our community has been horribly affected. So many lives were impacted that day."

"Go on, Zoey," I urged, knowing there was still more to tell.

"I'm not a religious person. I never even heard of a medium and didn't know anything about spirit contact. But somehow I felt drawn to it. It wasn't a choice; it was my survival. Just reading scripture about heaven didn't bring me any relief. I needed to know more. I had to make this connection to know if there is more to life than this," she explained.

"You seem to have quite an in-depth understanding," I complimented.

"I've done a lot of work to get to this point." She shook her head. "And it hasn't even been a year yet. I've learned to meditate. And while I can't do what you do, I do feel the presence of my children near me."

"Everyone is capable of having a mediumistic experience," I shared.

"Yes, but not everyone is a medium—I know that. I read your book *Never Letting Go*," Zoey replied.

"Wait! I'm hearing more from the children. The spirits of Jordan and Jada want me to convey something else to you," I told her.

"What makes me angry," Zoey interrupted, "is that he has access to my children and I don't!"

"Interesting you should say that," I replied. "Because their message is, 'We can see Daddy when we want to.'"

"Could you ask them to explain that, please?"

"This is astonishing! Jordan and Jada say they're on a higher level." I was genuinely surprised.

"Can you tell me exactly what they are saying?" Zoey leaned toward me.

"Jordan and Jada say your husband is on a lower frequency on the Other Side. He is in a place devoid of the happiness your children feel. He is atoning for his crime—this unspeakable act he committed. He may eventually emerge from this level but not until he is ready."

"I do believe he has created his own hell," Zoey said. "He now knows and fully comprehends what he has done. And I know I have to get to forgiving him, but I'm just not ready yet."

"In a sense, you're right. He is in a type of hell. It's where he must constantly reflect on what he's done. He relives it over and over," I described.

Zoey sat silently.

"There's more. Jordan and Jada can adjust their vibrations to a lower frequency to be with him when they choose—but he cannot adjust his vibration to a higher frequency to see them. Literally, he is on a lower frequency—and one without the ability to ascend to the higher level where your children are." I stopped to listen. "Now your children are taking me to a different place."

"Where?" Zoey seemed excited.

"They are on a lake. I see them on a sailboat. I feel the cool breeze on my face, the fresh smell of the water. Jada is at the bow of the boat. Jordan is in the rear, throwing rocks into the water and laughing. They both want you to know they are free and happy and—goodness, this is peculiar…"

"Tell me!" she implored.

"Their message is, 'We will be back.'" I reported.

"I understand all of that completely," Zoey said. "First, my daughter Jada was crazy about the water. I could never get her out of the pool. She loved to look at the sailboats on the lakes near where we lived. And both my children loved to sit on the dock next to the lake and throw rocks in the water. My son especially liked to watch the expanding concentric circles that developed when he threw a rock into it."

"You said you understand the message 'we will be back.' What does that mean to you?" I asked.

"Well, I've always wondered about reincarnation," Zoey replied, "and I've come to believe in it. I've asked God if they will come back here someday—and now I have my answer."

Zoey and I were amazed that her children had so completely and concisely explained about levels on the Other Side in a way we could understand. The images of Jordan and Jada on the sailboat and the immense happiness they were experiencing indicate they are in the heaven dimension of the Other Side.

It is impossible for us in the finite material world to fully comprehend the infinity of the Other Side. We are physical, and spirits are pure energy. Based on my experience and interaction with spirits, it appears that when spirits project an image of themselves in a familiar bucolic setting, they are providing us with a point of reference we can understand.

This may be compared to a PhD in science trying to explain Einstein's Theory of Relativity to children in kindergarten. Although some of the children may be equipped with great intellect, those children still lack the experience and education to fully grasp Einstein's concepts. That is why the PhD would have to give examples that are easy to understand without going into the extreme technical details.

In Zoey's reading, her children projected to me the image of something they loved to do, which she immediately recognized. It was her children's love of the water, sailing, and even their love of throwing rocks into the water. Because of these images, she understood how happy Jordan and Jada are. The spirits of her children reached out to her to give her a glimpse of the eternal nature of life. These specific images were provided so that their mother would find some measure of inner peace by understanding that they are in heaven.

On the other hand, Kurtis, their father and murderer, resides in a totally different frequency. Although he can see his children, he cannot do so unless they agree to visit him. His children have forgiven him on the Other Side, yet he must now atone for what he has done. In Catholic terms, it is a type of purgatory. It is not an eternal state of torment; rather, it is an absence of the peace and happiness of the Light.

This purgatory dimension of the Other Side was not a place of torture inflicted upon Kurtis by a vengeful God or by demons but by his own spirit. It is his place of reflection, where he must relive and revisit what he has done. Eventually his spirit will have the opportunity to emerge from this level and rise to a higher vibration. This is achieved through atoning, resolving, and assisting other spirits, and through reincarnation, where his spirit returns to the material world in human form.

As an attorney, I have to wonder from a legal standpoint if the fact that Kurtis was mentally disturbed has a bearing upon his state in the purgatory dimension. What father in his right mind could commit such atrocities? Did he completely understand what he was doing? Should he not be forgiven or found not guilty by reason of insanity? It is very human to analyze the infinite Other Side on the basis of my limited material world experiences. I can only relate what I observe and realize that my limited human understanding cannot answer these questions. That is reserved for God.

5

The Other Side and the Collective Consciousness Disconnect

Our earth's oceans may be a way for us to understand or possibly catch a preview of the Other Side's eternal nature. The ocean has many different levels. Near the surface of the water, closest to the light, we find an abundant array of life and color. However, the deeper one goes into the sea, the more the light diminishes, the temperature plummets, and the pressure becomes immense. Yet life exists even in the darkest depths of the ocean floor, and despite its diverse levels, the ocean remains a vast, interconnected body of water.

Likewise, the Other Side has many different levels and is a collective consciousness, where everyone and everything is interconnected energetically. Within this interconnectedness, there are an infinite number of levels and frequencies.

When a person dies, his or her energy is released from the material world confines of the body. That spirit is energy and may be analogized to a drop of water. That drop of water has its own individual uniqueness.

The transitional process we know as death causes the drop of water to enter an infinite ocean. Now the drop of water has become part of something vastly larger than itself. The drop has become part of the ocean of infinity we can call the Other Side.

"Is my loved one alone?" I am frequently asked this question. The answer is no. A collective consciousness means that spirits are all part of an infinite energetic connection. No one is ever alone. There may be different levels and frequencies, and not all spirits have access to all of these levels and frequencies, but no one is ever totally isolated.

DURING A READING for Kirk, his father's spirit came through. As a medium I've learned to "give what I get," no matter how bizarre it may seem. The reason for this is that if

I don't, then I may miss a crucial piece of evidence communicated by the spirit.

"*Klaatu barada nikto*," I conveyed. "Kirk, I know that phrase! Isn't it from that science-fiction movie *The Day the Earth Stood Still?*"

"That was Dad's favorite movie!" Kirk exclaimed.

It was hard for me not to smile. First, I felt a sense of relief that something so off-the-wall meant so much to Kirk. Secondly, it was ironic because, in the movie, a visitor from another world used the phrase.

"Can I ask Dad a question?" Kirk asked.

"Sure," I replied.

"What's heaven—you know, the Other Side—like?" Kirk wanted to know.

Although clients ask this question quite a bit, I am always curious to learn more about the Other Side from spirits. Spirits communicate from the Other Side very much like they did when they were alive. In physical life Kirk's dad was an extremely intellectual man, and he came through from the Other Side in just that manner.

"It is a collective consciousness but where there is detachment. We are all connected and able to communicate with a vast number of other spirits, but we retain our individuality. And we can detach from it should we need to."

"Whoa—that is fascinating," Kirk said.

"It is indeed," I said, overwhelmed by his father's succinct and enlightening description.

FROM MY ONGOING work with spirits, it appears to me that every being in the universe is interconnected energetically in one vast, infinite ocean that transcends dimension, frequency, space, and time. I'd never met Hunter prior to conducting a reading for him. His was a tragic love story. Soon after Hunter proposed to Elise, she was diagnosed with cancer; it took her life within weeks. Hunter was understandably devastated. Nearly a year after her passing, he contacted me.

Elise communicated a tremendous amount of evidence to Hunter. It was a pleasure to work with a spirit who was so forthcoming. Midway through the reading, the connection took on a new sensation. Although her presence remained warm and loving, I felt her energy strengthen. I was somewhat overwhelmed due to this sensory overload but I went with it, knowing Elise needed to convey something important to Hunter.

"She loved a great view," I blurted, trying to adjust to this growing level of energy. "I'm seeing the sunset over the ocean. I feel the ebb and flow of the tide."

"We used to sit on my sailboat and watch the sunset together," Hunter explained.

"It's clear she loved the view of the sunset because it was beautiful and romantic, but there's more! My God! I've never felt this before!"

"Mark, are you okay?" Hunter asked. "You sound like this is really taxing on you."

"Hunter, this is more than just a shared memory of something the two of you enjoyed. She is kicking it up a few levels!" The surge of energy flowing though my body intensified.

"What's happening?" Hunter wanted to know.

"I feel great—amazing, actually! Wow! She's letting me know what she feels like where she is now. It is an intense feeling of love and serenity. This is what I call the heaven dimension! And I not only feel the ebb and flow of the tide of the ocean when you two were on the sailboat, but now—now she is letting me feel what it is like to separate from the material confines of a body."

"Oh, man! Go for it!" Hunter cried out. His elation was obvious.

"It's uncanny—I actually feel my consciousness shifting up and away from my body—only I'm seeing and feeling things from Elise's perspective."

"Explain!" Hunter couldn't hide his excitement.

"I'm feeling things as she does!"

"Wow!" Hunter exclaimed. "Tell me more!"

"I'm feeling like I'm hovering above the water—and at the same time, it's like I've melded with the water—except it feels like the water is energy and I'm part of that energy," I described.

Hunter was speechless.

"At the same time, I feel connected to the sky—to the air itself—also energy but with a lighter feel to it," I explained. "And now her energy is speeding up! I'm connected to the water—to the air—to the sky—it's like being in more than one place at the same time!" Even though I felt light and uplifted, my heartbeat intensified, and I felt heat surging through my body.

"Elise says this is being part of everything, everywhere—a collective consciousness; so many minds and thoughts touching each other, together and yet separate. For her it isn't overwhelming; it is peaceful and exciting and joyous at the same time. She is part of everything! She is part of everything, everywhere, but still herself—her own unique self. It is amazing! It is being—it is total connection to the universe…and more than the universe—that word is too limiting. It is total being—total existence!"

Suddenly the sensation separated, and I returned to the awareness of my own body.

Hunter was flabbergasted. "That was pretty cool!" he exclaimed.

"Hunter, I feel so privileged! For a few seconds she let me feel what it is like to touch heaven's veil, meaning connected to everything! I saw Elise completely in tune with the rhythm of the energy that is all around us. It was a beautiful, empowering, and energetic experience all at once. I guess that is what is meant by being one with the universe."

Other mediums have told me they've had similar experiences during contact with spirits. My colleagues agree it is a humbling experience and at the same time a gift to feel, if only for a few seconds, what it is like to be pure spiritual energy.

LIKE THE DROPS of water composing the ocean, our individual spirits are all cells in the energetic body of God. When spirits need to emerge as an individual to communicate with someone in the material world or to accomplish a mission on the Other Side, they can disconnect from the collective consciousness.

Perhaps God's greatest gift to us is our own sense of self. It separates us from everyone and everything else in the universe. It gives each of us our individuality. It makes our personal experiences in life unique. We each have our own thoughts, memories, feelings, and perspectives.

What do we do with this uniqueness? The Hindus and Buddhists believe that the key to happiness is elimination of the self. This does not mean the elimination of who you are. Rather, it is the removal of selfishness, desire, and the unending craving for material or emotional needs.

Jesus taught us to love others as we love ourselves. In so doing, one does not put one's self ahead of everyone else. Rather, one brings everyone to an equal parity with the self and thereby eliminates selfishness.

While a sense of self is truly a gift, it also remains the ultimate test of our character. Do we embrace and cherish our individuality and share ourselves with others? Or do we see our self as the center of the universe, excluding others as unworthy? The choice is ours.

This sense of self is what makes us truly unique. And nothing—not even death—can remove that uniqueness.

6

Interdimensional Communication

Some will say that there is no way anyone can communicate with a spirit—that it's impossible.

Impossible? Just because something is outside the realm of one's personal experience does not mean it is impossible.

The Other Side is a dimension separate from the material world dimension in which we reside. A medium is a person who is sensitive to the ultra-high frequencies of the Other

Side. Like a radio, he or she is the medium—that is, the conduit or transmission tool through which information from the Other Side is conveyed. Interdimensional communication—the transference of information between these two dimensions—is not only possible but readily accessible.

It never ceases to astound me that there are those who will summarily reject the reality of spirit communication just because they have no experience or understanding of it. This is especially ironic because every day we take for granted technology and other forms of communication that seem impossible, even miraculous, to those who do not have access to it.

I was fortunate to be part of a photographic expedition of the Amazon River in Peru aboard *La Esmeralda*, a ninety-foot-long research vessel carrying about two dozen passengers and crew. The ship had three decks, with the uppermost deck serving as an open-air observation platform. The passengers were American; the crew consisted of Amazonian natives.

La Esmeralda embarked from the port of Iquitos in the Peruvian Amazon. Although Iquitos is a large and heavily populated city, it is a secluded port that can only be reached by boat or airplane. It is a truly distinctive city with a unique culture, home to hundreds of thousands of impoverished people.

After leaving Iquitos, *La Esmeralda* cruised to the remote reaches of the Amazon rainforest. What we consider civilization quickly vanished as the ship entered the deep recesses of the massive river. A strikingly beautiful primordial world colored a thousand shades of green, the Amazon is a photographer's paradise. Its dark waters abound with fish, freshwater dolphins, and a species of alligator known as caiman. The dense jungle is home to myriad rare and mysterious creatures, including prehistoric-looking mammals, flocks of colorful birds, swarms of immense insects, and huge snakes.

The villages we visited were extremely primitive by our standards. Running water and electricity were unknown, as were telephones, radios, and other forms of technology requiring electricity. The native Amazonians were very friendly and seemed happy. They appeared as fascinated by us as we were with them.

It was such an honor to meet and learn from the native peoples of the Amazon. Their deep love and respect for their natural home was inspiring. They saw themselves not only as inhabitants of the Amazon but organic to it. Our guide and translator, Juan, explained how his people believed that the energy of all life is interconnected. "We are more than inhabitants of the Amazon," he explained. "We are as much a part of the Amazon as the waters of the great river itself."

Unlike the natives in the remote villages we visited, the crew of *La Esmeralda* lived in Iquitos and had access to telephones, radios, and television. This piqued their desire to learn more about the technology that we in the United States take for granted.

One evening, just as darkness was falling, the vessel anchored for the night. The sky was cloudless; with no electric lights for hundreds of miles, the stars appeared enormous. The dark waters of the Amazon were as still as a mirror, capturing the brilliant reflection of the stars above.

Suddenly, one of the crew cried out as he pointed up to the sky. The rest of the crew hurried to the upper observation deck and looked skyward in awe. A bright orb of light silently traversed the night sky from west to east in a horizontal trajectory. Our guide, Juan, translated what the men were saying.

"There it is: the star that never falls!"

"That's a satellite," I said. "My father was a NASA engineer and worked on them."

"Satellite! What is that?" Juan asked as a crowd gathered around to hear what I had to say.

I felt self-conscious and overwhelmed as they all gazed at me. "It's a machine that orbits the earth. It conveys radio and telephone transmissions from one part of the earth to another," I explained.

"Airplanes make sound—why does it make no sound?" another crew member wanted to know.

"How did the machine get to heaven?" another man asked.

"Why does it never fall?" inquired another.

These men were not familiar with satellites and wanted to know more about them. I've never had a more open-minded and eager group of students. They were fascinated to learn everything I could tell them about space travel. My dad was a NASA engineer and one of the men who figured out how to bring Apollo 13 safely back to earth. I did my best to recall what my dad had taught me about satellites. Needless to say, it was a long night as their questions continued for hours.

COMMUNICATION THROUGH TRANSFERENCE of energy is a fact of life in the modern world. For example, if you live in Santa Barbara, California, and use your cell phone to call your Aunt Martha in Liverpool, England, did you realize this involves a tremendous amount of equipment and energetic transfers?

The decision you make to call Aunt Martha is an energetic impulse generated in your brain. This impulse is converted into mechanical energy as your vocal cords vibrate. This vibrational energy is now transferred into radio wave energy that is transmitted to a tower, converting it into electrical energy. This energy travels to an antenna and is beamed via radio waves bouncing off a network of satellites orbiting the earth.

This radio wave energy is then beamed to an antenna in England and converted back into electrical energy, which becomes sound-wave energy as it is received by Aunt Martha's phone. This sound-wave energy enters Aunt Martha's ear and causes her eardrum to vibrate. This vibration is transferred back into electrical energy and translated by her brain into "hello, Aunt Martha!"

And we get irritated when our cell phone calls drop out unexpectedly!

A century and a half ago, a small box from which human-sounding voices emerged was only a theory. Two centuries ago, it would've been deemed witchcraft. Clearly, a cell phone call is not witchcraft. It is a form of communication based on the transfer of energy involving frequency and vibration.

Since energy can neither be created nor destroyed, only transferred, it takes a lot of equipment and energetic conversions to accomplish what we consider everyday communication—a telephone call.

Thomas Edison, one of the world's greatest inventors and geniuses, theorized that a telephone call to the Other Side was possible. He speculated that a device sensitive enough to tune in to the ultra-high frequency of spirits—the so-called spirit phone—could be created. Unfortunately, Edison did not live long enough to fully develop the spirit phone.

Interdimensional communication, or communication between people here in the material world and spirits on the Other Side, is also based on the transfer of energy involving frequency and vibration. In some ways it is less complex than a cell phone call, yet it is not without its complications. Like a telephone call, it also requires "equipment" to enable the communication to occur.

There is a physiological basis to spirit communication centered on the pineal gland within the brain. The pineal gland is a pea-sized endocrine gland located behind the center of the forehead. For those who practice yoga, this is the third eye chakra (chakras are energy centers within the human body). Endocrine glands produce and secrete hormones directly into the bloodstream. The locations of the chakras coincide with the locations of the endocrine glands within the human body.

The pineal gland is highly complex and has many functions. It regulates our physical and mental activity levels during a twenty-four-hour cycle, produces the hormone melatonin, and is instrumental in how humans process light.

All the great spiritual teachers have described God as "Light." People who have had a near-death experience often describe entering the Light and being surrounded by a loving presence and infinite intelligence. Perhaps light is the manner in which humans are able to perceive God's spiritual energy. The pineal gland may be the equipment that enables us to perceive more than just the light of the visible spectrum.

A British-German study conducted by professors Serena Roney-Dougal and Gunther Vogl discovered how the pineal gland produces psychoactive hormones that appear connected to psychic and mediumistic activity.

A French-Israeli study conducted by doctors Simon Baconnier, Sidney Lang, and Rene De Seze revealed the presence of calcite and magnetite crystals within the pineal gland. Both of these crystals generate an electrical charge. Magnetite has an electromagnetic field.

Early radios were basically a crystal attached to a copper wire—henceforth, a crystal radio. Theoretically, the pineal gland may serve as both an antenna and a transmitter. As such, it appears the pineal gland is the physiological basis for a human's ability to "tune in" to frequencies from the Other Side. In other words, we human beings have an extremely sophisticated radio station in our heads.

How does all of this equipment in our heads work so we can talk to spirits? As a medium, I do not summon or conjure spirits. I voluntarily allow myself to be sensitive to frequency.

I was born with this ability, and I've worked to understand and enhance it. To communicate with a spirit, a medium must raise his or her frequency and vibrational energy as a spirit lowers his or hers in order for both parties to obtain a frequency and vibrational energy match.

It's a lot like tuning in to a radio station. Think of an FM radio dial. Our material world station is at a lower rate of frequency—for example, 89.5 on the FM dial. Spirits are on a higher frequency, so their station might be 107.9. The medium raises frequency as a spirit lowers frequency, and the two try to reach a station somewhere in between, perhaps 100.7. When this is achieved, interdimensional communication—contact between the material world dimension and the Other Side—is achieved.

During interdimensional communication, a medium's energy field interfaces with the spirit's, enabling the medium to discern information from the spirit's energy field. Spirits vibrate concepts in energetic waves that are received by the medium and converted into electric energy in the form of thoughts, feelings, and sensations. The medium then translates these into recognizable human concepts.

We all have the same "equipment," which is why everyone is capable of having a mediumistic experience even though everyone is not a medium. Some people are simply better able to connect than others. It is my belief that mediums are born, not made. Perhaps it is based on physiological factors not yet fully understood, like having an extra calcite or magnetite crystal in the pineal gland. Each of us is unique, with different gifts and abilities. Some are great athletes, yet those who can swim may not win a gold medal in the Olympics for swimming. Many can sing, but not everyone is pitch perfect. We can probably all understand physics to some degree, yet how many of us truly understand the theories of Albert Einstein?

However, like all forms of communication, interdimensional communication can be affected by energetic interference. Telephones, television, computers, the Internet—all of them fail from time to time. Sometimes your favorite radio station is easy to tune in to and other times it isn't. There may be static or interference or there may be a problem with the radio. Likewise, during spirit contact, sometimes the link with the Other Side is more direct than at other times. Communication with a spirit is invigorating, and it is also physically draining. The medium may be having a bad day, or the person for whom the message is intended may be blocking the contact.

If a client approaches a reading with a negative attitude or, conversely, is intensely desirous of spirit contact, both of these behaviors can result in the creation of an energy barrier. A bad attitude seldom achieves good results. Also, if an atmosphere of "I want" is present, that can inadvertently create a block for the energetic transfer from the Other Side.

My belief is that intense desire is energetically similar to a bad attitude. I've conducted thousands of readings and find that the best interdimensional communication occurs when the client lets go of wanting and instead simply welcomes the contact. Spirit contact works well when both the medium and the client are relaxed. The "I want" perspective is an ego-based function. It is best when "I want this contact" is reframed as "I welcome this contact." This removes an energetic block to interdimensional communication.

Mediumship, or the ability to engage in interdimensional communication, is a gift from God. It allows us to know that life is everlasting and that our loved ones did not disintegrate at their physical death. Energy is neither created nor destroyed—it is only transferred. When someone dies, that person's energy is transferred to a different form on a different frequency in a different dimension.

COMMUNICATION WITH THE Other Side through a medium is nothing new. It has been reported since the dawn of recorded history. Unfortunately, a lot of primitive superstitions surround interdimensional communication. People tend to fear what they do not understand—or what they feel threatens their belief system. This is why some believe negative energies, evil spirits, or demons are behind those things they cannot comprehend. I've seen this not only in the US but also in the Amazon.

A few days after explaining my layman's understanding of satellites and space travel to the crew of *La Esmeralda*, we cruised up a branch of the Amazon known as Rio Ucayali and anchored about a mile from a small village of thatched-roof huts. The crew handed each of us a bamboo pole with a string and hook attached and told us we were to fish for piranhas for our evening meal.

"Seriously?" I asked Juan, our guide.

"*Sí*—I mean yes. They are good to eat," he responded with a slight laugh.

"I never thought about eating piranhas, but I have to admit, I am afraid of being eaten *by* them," I commented.

Juan translated my remark to the crew, who found it outrageously funny. Juan was a good-natured man, and he explained how a lot of fear surrounds piranhas because people don't really understand them. Despite Juan's informative explanation about these fish with enormous teeth, I had to admit that my perceptions of the black waters of the Rio Ucayali are still colored by Hollywood-induced images of falling overboard into a frothing school of voracious piranhas waiting to strip me to the bone in seconds.

While we were talking, several canoes approached *La Esmeralda* carrying about twenty natives from the nearby village. The locals were excited and carried on an enthusiastic conversation with the crew. My fellow American passengers gathered on the deck near Juan so we could find out what was going on.

"El Brujo!" the crew kept repeating.

"What is that?" I asked Juan.

"The witch doctor. The witch doctor is in the village, and he wants to see you," Juan said ominously.

"Me?" I asked.

"All of you, but you most of all—the one who talks to ghosts," Juan told me. "That is how the crew speaks of you." Apparently, the crew had given me a nickname.

Juan explained how the witch doctor had heard of me from villagers many miles away. Apparently, several days earlier, the crew told the residents of another village that a medium was aboard *La Esmeralda*. Word of the "one who talks to ghosts" spread rapidly through the region. Gossip, it seems, is as prevalent in the Amazon as it is anywhere else.

La Esmeralda hoisted its anchor and made the short voyage to the village. On the way, Juan told us that El Brujo had come a long way by canoe to this village to perform an exorcism. Evil spirits had possessed a young woman in the village. El Brujo had been summoned from another village to cast out these devils.

Two of my traveling companions—Arlene, a botanist in her late forties, and Nigel, a retired orthopedic surgeon in his early seventies—were just as intrigued as I was to observe a native spiritual ritual. The other passengers were somewhat reluctant to walk into the middle of an exorcism.

Night began to fall upon the hot and humid rainforest as we entered the small village. Without electricity and in the dark, what had seemed so picturesque aboard *La Esmeralda* now took on a menacing character.

A crowd of about a hundred natives surrounded El Brujo when we approached the large bamboo hut with a thatched roof where the exorcism was to be performed. The witch doctor appeared quite different from what I had expected.

For some reason, my stereotypical notion had been that he'd be scantily clad, wearing only an elaborate feathered headdress and loincloth—and have chicken bones piercing his nose. Instead, he was about fifty years old and clean-shaven, with short salt-and-pepper hair. Like all of the villagers, he was barefoot but wearing a white cotton shirt, baseball cap, and weathered jeans. I somehow felt he should've been called Fred instead of El Brujo. I bit my tongue to suppress a laugh.

El Brujo was delighted we were in attendance. Juan translated for us. He wanted outsiders—Americans—to see this important ritual. He told Juan he was honored that the one who talks to ghosts had arrived. I was humbled when El Brujo bowed to me, and I bowed back out of respect.

Standing outside a woven palm-frond mat that served as the door to the hut, El Brujo explained that this was going to be a delicate, difficult exorcism and we must be on guard lest the demons leave her and enter us. He pushed the mat aside and beckoned us to enter the bamboo hut.

It was dark inside save for a small fire, which illuminated the faces of the people awaiting El Brujo. The floor of the hut was made of wooden planks; the walls were constructed of bamboo covered with palm fronds. A terrified woman named Cara lay face down on a thin mattress stuffed with leaves. She looked to be about thirty years old. Two young, very muscular men and an older woman knelt on the floor beside her. They were Cara's immediate family members—her husband, her brother, and her mother.

The family positioned itself in a semicircle on one side of the hut with El Brujo in the center beside Cara. Our group was asked to kneel in a semicircular position on the other side of the hut. Arlene, the botanist, was on my right, and Nigel, the orthopedic surgeon, was to my left. All of us had our cameras ready.

El Brujo threw some herbs on the fire. When they began to smolder, they smelled similar to sage. The air grew pungent. I noticed I wasn't the only one whose eyes began to water.

Juan translated. "El Brujo says Cara is possessed by demons."

Suddenly, what started as an adventure became intensely intimidating. Although I do not believe in the devil, at least not in the traditional sense, an overwhelming fear gripped my body and I broke out into a cold sweat.

Irrational thoughts raced through my head: What if there really is a devil? What if this woman actually is possessed by the devil? We're in the middle of nowhere! No one knows we're here! What if the demons come after me? I'm a medium—will I be more susceptible? Can I deflect them? Am I about to come face to face with the Prince of Darkness?

All the childhood fears of my Catholic upbringing emerged from the recesses of my mind. Fear flooded through me, and I was overwhelmed by the fight-or-flight response. I wanted to run.

Yet, as a Catholic, I'd also been taught to "fear not." As an adult, I understand that my religion is about being a spiritual, studious, open-minded individual—one who never surrenders to fear but instead has faith in God. I am an attorney, a man of logic, and, more importantly, a man of faith. My faith has led me to study and respect all of the world's great religious teachings. My interfaith approach has strengthened my belief in God, who transcends all fear. I knew I must turn to faith.

For me, the devil is a metaphor for the struggle between the light and the darkness within—what we know is right versus our own ego-driven, self-centered desires. I've come to know that we don't need a jerk with a pitchfork to make us commit evil acts. I reminded myself that whenever someone is cruel and sinful, it is not because he or she is acting in the Light of spirituality. Rather, he or she is embracing the darkness of impulsive animalistic desires, base-level aggression, and pure selfishness.

In this remote village in the Amazon, I abandoned rationality in favor of fear—simply because I was confronted by the unknown. Suddenly, the words of my mother, Jeannie, came to me: "Even the deepest darkness cannot stand up to one ray of light. Light paves the way to understanding and truth." Mom was a psychic medium as well as a devout Catholic. She taught me that the best solution in times of fear and doubt is prayer. Kneeling there between my travel companions, I closed my eyes and, despite the acrid smoke, took a deep breath. Silently, I said a prayer and visualized being surrounded by the white Light of God.

A sense of calm came over me. I felt infused with an inner peace. My childhood fears of the unknown melted away. With a new mental and spiritual clarity, I felt free of the presence of any malevolent spirits.

Meanwhile, El Brujo had begun the exorcism. He knelt beside Cara on the floor, with a number of small bottles containing liquid or powder nearby.

Juan translated the witch doctor's diagnosis. "El Brujo says the demons are creating pain in her body and along her back."

El Brujo began to chant in a native dialect. He poured one of the liquids on Cara's back and mixed in a few powders, then paused. Finally, he poured a syrupy liquid on the area of her back that he deemed to be the epicenter of demonic activity.

Cameras flashed. El Brujo beamed with delight that the outsiders were documenting his work. He described each step so Juan could translate. This Amazonian witch doctor took as much pride in explaining his skill as a Harvard Medical School professor might in teaching us about the latest surgical techniques. His concern for Cara was sincere and touching. This man was a healer, and I truly admired him.

El Brujo continued to pour additional liquids and powders on Cara's back, stirring them together into a gluelike consistency. Periodically, he looked upward and chanted loudly. After a pause, El Brujo leaned forward, affixing his mouth on Cara's back. For several minutes, he made lapping and slurping sounds as he sucked the substance into his mouth.

Then he sat bolt upright and spat a huge gelatinous glob into the palm of his right hand. The dark, viscous syrup dribbled down his chin as the bulk of it oozed through his fingers.

"Ugh! That's disgusting," whispered Nigel's wife, who looked like she was about to vomit.

Then El Brujo sat staunchly upright and ceremoniously flung the gooey slop into the fire, which began to sputter. Juan translated El Brujo's proclamation. He announced, "The demon has been exorcised! I sucked it from her and cast it into the fire of shadows!"

Cara's family clasped hands. Proudly, El Brujo sat up tall.

"Cara isn't possessed," Nigel, the surgeon, murmured to me. "That woman has a herniated disk. In my forty years as an orthopedic surgeon, I've seen these cases thousands of times. It looks like it's in the mid to lower lumbar region of her spine. It's very painful. Most likely she needs surgery."

"Fat chance of that happening here," Arlene said softly.

"So when pain is caused by something they don't understand, they think it's a demon." I nodded at Nigel.

"Well, a herniated disk hurts like the devil—but no, it's not a demon!" Nigel confirmed.

I glanced from Nigel back to El Brujo, who was staring at me as Juan began to translate. "Did you see the demons leave her, one who talks to ghosts?"

I hesitated as all eyes in the hut were upon me. Although the hut was thick with humidity and acrid smoke, the tension in the air seemed even heavier. Oddly, it felt a lot like being in court waiting for a verdict—except this time, I was the one delivering the verdict.

El Brujo waited for my reply with a judicial demeanor. Yet the jury I knelt before appeared even more judgmental. Cara's dark brown eyes expressed terror as she looked up at me from the floor. Her husband and brother stared at me intensely. Cara's mother clasped her hands in prayer, tears streaming from her eyes. My American friends looked anxious, clearly hoping I wouldn't say something offensive to a witch doctor in a remote jungle village while surrounded by a hundred superstitious natives.

"I sense there are no demons here," I answered.

Cara and her family cheered. El Brujo sat up straight and smiled. The Americans looked relieved.

"Well said, one who talks to ghosts," Nigel said, shaking my hand.

"El Brujo will now prevent the demon from returning with protective magic," Juan translated as the witch doctor removed a small bundle of what appeared to be weeds from a pouch.

El Brujo began to thrash Cara's back with the weeds. The young woman clenched her fists, wincing in pain.

"Oh no! He can't be serious," Arlene whispered to me as Cara flinched again at the painful sensation. El Brujo continued his lashing.

"Good heavens!" Nigel exclaimed as ugly red welts formed on Cara's back.

"Arlene, what is that plant?" I asked, distressed by Cara's groans. The welts on her back grew larger.

"It's a rare form of poison ivy, indigenous to the Amazon. It's extremely toxic," Arlene said softly.

When Cara's back was completely red and swollen, El Brujo stopped abruptly. He looked over to us for approval and smiled. Awkwardly, we smiled back. Cara may not have been possessed by demons, but at this moment she looked like hell.

"She will feel better in a week!" Juan translated the witch doctor's prognosis.

"She couldn't feel worse!" Arlene whispered.

"One thing is certain," Nigel explained when we were safely back aboard *La Esmeralda*. "In a week she'll still have the herniated disk. Once the discomfort and swelling caused by the poison ivy subsides, the pain she has now will seem to have lessened, and then she'll think she's better—at least for a time."

"Yes, until the demons return," Arlene added, rolling her eyes.

"On the other hand," I explained to Arlene, "Cara might feel better because El Brujo gave her something everyone suffering and frightened needs: hope."

PEOPLE TEND TO fear what they do not understand. For the Amazonian natives, Cara's herniated lumbar disk was caused by something beyond their understanding. To treat it with modern medical technology would be outside their realm of experience or comprehension. Because they could not understand the cause of her injury, they feared it. For them it was natural to conclude that pain without a visible sign of injury was caused by demonic possession.

Ignorance and superstition are the tools of fear. The fear-generated superstition of those who do not understand interdimensional communication often surrounds mediums. Even though we are all physiologically equipped to sense and perceive the presence of spirits, not everyone is willing to accept it as a reality.

Over the centuries, the enlightened teachings of the great spiritual masters have often been manipulated by religious leaders to create fear. Fear is a human means of manipulation and control. There are those who see interdimensional communication, commonly referred to as a reading by a medium, as the work of demons. They fear a direct connection with the spiritual energy of the Other Side because they feel it threatens what they proclaim to be the one and only way to heaven. Access to heaven and the perception of God is individual, personal, and for everyone, not for a select group of clerics and their particular dogmas, rituals, and need for financial support.

God exists in spite of religion, not because of religion. That is not to say that religion is a negative thing; quite the contrary. God is infinite, and religions represent our finite means of understanding and perceiving God. More importantly, religions teach peace and love. Truly, we must love one another as we love ourselves and treat each other as we wish to be treated. When religion is hijacked and used as a moral justification for anger, bigotry, fear, hatred, or violence, then it ceases to be about God and becomes an instrument of the human ego.

Interdimensional communication is a gift from God and is not to be feared. In the thousands of readings I've conducted, my observation is that spirit communication brings healing and comfort to those suffering with the loss of a loved one. This gift has been given to humanity to enable us to understand the everlasting nature of life.

There is nothing magical about this kind of communication. Its reality comes from the physiological equipment known as the pineal gland, which we all have. Like the everyday technology of telephones, radios, televisions, and the Internet, our equipment enables us to connect with a distant place through frequency and energetic transfers. This equipment enables us to be sensitive to the spiritual presence of loved ones and to perceive, if only for a moment, the Light of God.

7

Multiple-Meaning Messages

The process of learning spans a lifetime—and then some. A baby doesn't come into this world fluent in language. The child must first learn to recognize intelligent communication transmitted by sound waves as representative of concepts, feelings, expressions, facts, and data. It takes more time for that child to learn to talk. Speech is the ability to intelligently communicate concepts through the use of sound waves. However, speech is just the first step. It takes even longer still for a child to understand the nuances, double meanings, and subtleties of language.

We use words every day that have multiple meanings—and so do spirits in the messages they communicate from the Other Side. Interdimensional communication does not consist simply of perceiving symbols, images, songs, feelings, sensations, or numbers conveyed by a spirit. It requires understanding that vibrations energetically transmitted by a spirit are often loaded with a tremendous amount of information. When the recipient of the messages in the material world comprehends the full scope of the communication, the result is a more significant message from a loved one on the Other Side.

Part of honing one's interdimensional communication is becoming familiar with the language of spirit communication. Messages from the Other Side may contain more information than just what is initially perceived. Part of this is in understanding multiple-meaning messages.

During a reading, for example, a medium receives evidence from a spirit. A piece of evidence may be transmitted in the form of an image, word, sound, impression, or sensation. A multiple-meaning message occurs when a piece of information contains more than one level of information. Like communication in the material world, interdimensional communication contains nuances, subtleties, and words with several connotations.

Multiple-meaning messages are more than just acknowl-edging that an image or word has more than one meaning. It is an understanding of how spirits transmit information during interdimensional communication, which bears a strik-ing similarity to radio transmissions among humans. For example, data communicated by radio, particularly in military circles, often requires transmission of secret encrypted messages. These encrypted messages are frequently piggy-backed on other messages of a seemingly nonsecretive nature. What this means is that even though a radio transmission appears to contain only one message, it actually contains multiple messages within that single transmission.

Similarly, when spirits emit waves of frequency to the medium, it often has more than one message embedded within it. When this happens, the most obvious message is the one that is generally accepted. However, upon closer examination, one may discover there are several levels of significance to an image or concept conveyed. In both material world communication and interdimensional communication, these additional bits of information must be carefully analyzed so the full scope and meaning of the messages may be understood.

It may take a time of reflection after a reading before the information received is fully comprehended. In other situations, multiple-meaning messages are quite obvious at the time the message is received. Like many messages received during interdimensional communication, multiple-meaning messages can be serious, emotionally intense, funny, and inspirational all at the same time.

MUSIC INFLUENCES MANY people. A particular song can have tremendous significance. Have you ever heard a song that evoked a powerful memory? Doesn't that memory bring up images, feelings, and emotions? Even if that event happened years earlier, doesn't it feel like it happened yesterday?

It is typical during interdimensional communication for music to come through. In fact, I get a lot of songs from spirits. When I start humming or singing during a reading, I'm not trying to be entertaining or perform cosmic karaoke. Songs suggest a year, a time frame, or an emotion. The message could be a line in a song or the song itself.

A gallery reading is a mediumship and interdimensional communication demonstration before a group of people. I've been filmed many times conducting readings. One such filming occurred during a gallery reading at Aquarian Dreams Metaphysical Center near Melbourne, Florida.

I was drawn to Rachel, an attractive woman in her late forties. When Rachel stood up and went to the microphone, a strong male presence came through to me. "Does the month of April—and the numbers 2 and 7 or 27—mean anything to you?" I asked.

"That's the day he died," Rachel responded.

In my mind's ear, I heard the Led Zeppelin hard rock classic "Rock and Roll" and started singing a few verses from the song.

"He actually sang that song at karaoke on our second date," Rachel shared.

"Who's Bob—Bob, Bob, Bob?" I asked as I received a strong wave of frequency.

"His name was Robert," Rachel answered quietly.

Robert's spirit continued to transmit the song. Although I'm a terrible dancer, the intensity of this energetic connection made me want to move with the music and start dancing. For a few moments I did, much to the crowd's amusement.

"Apparently he's still singing karaoke," I joked.

Rachel smiled as her eyes filled with tears.

The energetic link with Robert's spirit strengthened. He wanted me to hear the music but also to feel the emotions he was conveying through the music. As I realized this, the energy shifted to a deeper, more passionate level. I heard another song, this one by Stevie Wonder.

"He wants me to sing a song for you." I paused, took a deep breath, and sang one line from this touching love song.

Rachel began to weep. "We split up for a short time, and he moved back to Texas. I wouldn't take his phone calls—and one day when I came home, that was on my answering machine."

The line from Wonder's song "I Just Called to Say I Love You" was a multiple-meaning message. During the course of the reading, Robert indicated he was a guitarist. As a musician, songs were very important to him, and both of these songs were especially significant. The Led Zeppelin song evoked powerful memories of when they initially dated; the other brought back passionate remembrance of reconciliation after a separation.

However, the Stevie Wonder song had the deepest emotional impact. It is not only a beautiful love song, but it clearly expressed his love for her. Rachel had been the love of Robert's life and he had been hers, and selecting this song was very savvy on Robert's part. It was a way of letting her know love transcends physical death. As the conduit during this reading, I was literally able to convey to Rachel that Robert called to say he loved her once again.

IMAGES FROM MOVIES, television shows, and the actors in them have become part of our modern-day pop culture and can evoke powerful memories and feelings. This is why, in many readings, I see images of actors or scenes from movies and TV shows. Something about an actor or show may help me translate the vibrational frequency from a spirit into a recognizable image or concept for the person who requested the reading.

In a telephone reading I conducted for Brenda, the spirit of her mother made contact and presented multiple-meaning messages through the use of images of movies and actors.

"I'm seeing what looks like a clip from the old Bing Crosby movie *The Bells of St. Mary's*. It feels like an important image," I explained to Brenda.

"It is indeed!" she responded happily. "That was Mom's favorite movie."

"Super, but I think there's more to this message than just that. We need to take this one step at a time," I cautioned, realizing this looked like a multiple-meaning message.

"It is the only DVD I ever gave to Mom as a present," Brenda told me.

"Awesome!" I was excited as the multiple-meaning message began to unfold.

"And, Mom's name was Mary," she confided.

"Wow, this is wonderful," I said.

"I haven't been able to watch it since she died."

Clearly, this image had significance to Brenda.

"It was on TV just last week—two days before Christmas," Brenda added.

I took a deep breath.

"I sat and watched it by myself—and cried the whole way through it. Even though I cried, it made me feel somehow closer to Mom again—like she was watching the movie with me."

Brenda's mother knew that sending her a multiple-meaning message in the form of *The Bells of St. Mary's* was exactly what Brenda needed. Brenda immediately recognized all five levels of significance to the message. It was her mother's favorite movie, it was the only movie Brenda gave her mother as a present, her mother's name was Mary, Brenda couldn't watch the movie after her mother's passing, and finally she was able to watch the film even though it made her cry. Seeing the film was cathartic and an important step in Brenda's healing. The last part of the message also demonstrates how spirits know what is going on with us at a particular time.

It is my belief that when we're missing someone a lot, we send out a "frequency beacon." A frequency beacon is an energetic impulse created by our emotions. Spirits are sensitive to these beacons. When Brenda saw *The Bells of St. Mary's* was on television, the grief and sadness she carried as a result of her mother's death was a frequency beacon. It really reinforces the old saying "a picture is worth a thousand words." But in this case, it was worth a thousand memories—of love.

SOMETIMES DURING A reading, a spirit will transmit a message that makes sense to me right away. But I'm just the conduit for the message—it is the recipient of the message who matters during interdimensional communication. So if a message comes through and makes no sense to me but resonates with tremendous significance to the client, then I've done my job. The client is the reason the spirit is making the effort to communicate. It is all about sending forth messages of love, healing, and resolution.

Jonas is a filmmaker for a major film studio who contacted me for a phone reading. During the reading, the spirit of his father presented an interesting image.

"Bats—I see images of bats: not the bat you use in baseball but the creature. Is there some significance between your father and bats?" I asked. "I don't think he liked them, Jonas, but that's not unusual—a lot of people don't like bats. I'm getting some pretty strong feelings attached to this image."

"Dad had an issue with a bat: one got into his house. He never could stand them," Jonas answered.

"The image of bats is continuing, but this one isn't creepy, it's more—I know this sounds odd—loving," I conveyed, not fully comprehending the scope of the message.

"When Dad passed, I was overseas filming a movie," Jonas said.

"Well, he's still showing me bats—and wants you to know it's okay you weren't there," I relayed.

"I was in Transylvania filming this movie," Jonas explained.

"Ah, bats!" I exclaimed, finally realizing the connection.

"Bats!" Jonas echoed.

"Bats! Vampires! Vampire bats—ergo, Transylvania!" I said, amplifying the multiple-meaning message.

"Exactly! Bats meant a lot," Jonas confirmed.

"Your dad understood you had a job to do, and he's okay with that."

Jonas continued, "His health wasn't great when I left, but I figured he'd be fine. He told me not to worry—to go and do my job. But he died when I was overseas in Transylvania."

"I'm so sorry," I responded.

"Thank you, Mark, for letting me know he's okay about my not having been there for him."

"Thank your dad, Jonas—he's the one who knew bats would make that clear for you."

SPIRITS ARE ALWAYS around us; this is nothing to fear. Our loved ones on the Other Side are energetically connected to us, so they are aware of what is going on in our lives. When the opportunity presents itself, they like to let us know this, as Carole discovered by way of a multiple-meaning message.

"I feel the presence of a male spirit on your generational level—meaning a brother, cousin, or close friend. Very close—this person loved you, not in the romantic sense, but he loved you a lot."

"That's my brother, Gary," Carole said. "We were very close."

"Carole, do you remember I told you, prior to your reading, that I give what I get, no matter how bizarre?"

"You did indeed—so go ahead. I need to hear this," Carole replied.

"I'm seeing Little Red Riding Hood," I explained as I felt compelled to sing that song about being afraid of the Big Bad Wolf.

Carole chuckled. "That makes a lot of sense."

"Good, because I feel a bit ridiculous!" I confided. It is always comforting when something bizarre resonates with a client.

"This is highly metaphoric," I continued. "Your brother is conveying a message in which you're depicted as Little Red Riding Hood."

"Okay," Carole responded. "And?"

"You're struggling through the dark forest of life and trying your best to get through the fear that has always plagued you, which is a lot like what Little Red Riding Hood did, except that the fear culminated in reaching the safety and shelter of Grandma's house and finding that the Big Bad Wolf was hiding in disguise to ambush her." I described the meaning I was receiving from her brother.

"I have been plagued by fear my whole life," Carole acknowledged. "I tend to trust people I shouldn't. This makes sense to me."

"He's showing me more," I told Carole. Gary's spirit apparently liked to use colorful visual imagery. When he presented a concept, he let it unfold step by step. His concern for his sister's well-being reached out to her from the Other Side.

"You have conquered the fear," I reported, "by escaping from the false safe haven of Grandma's house into open green fields on a bright, sunny, carefree day."

"It's taken a long time and a lot of work, but I've learned to control my fear," Carole shared.

"This means even more," I continued. "Your brother says the image of an open field of green grass on a carefree day signifies what we're all looking for. It's an idealized notion of perfection, accomplishment, and safety. We think we need to go somewhere for happiness, but we must realize it's all within ourselves to begin with."

"Gary was so insightful," Carole said softly. "My brother's right—true peace and happiness do come from within."

"Interesting how he used the Big Bad Wolf as a means of describing your fear; it seems like a way of acknowledging that the fear emanated from your childhood," I conveyed.

"That's true—and it means a lot more than that!" Carole exclaimed.

"How so?"

"When you were talking about the Big Bad Wolf, I had to contain myself," Carole commented.

"Why?" I asked, eager to hear the answer.

"I didn't tell you before the reading what I do professionally. I'm a filmmaker, and I just finished shooting a movie about a werewolf. Gary's use of the Big Bad Wolf really cracks me up. That's so like him!"

These last two readings are good examples of the broad scope of multiple-meaning messages. The spirits in both readings conveyed vibrations that my brain translated into images that initially seemed creepy or scary: bats and wolves. On one level, they were. It would've been all too easy to focus just on their negative connotations instead of seeing how these spirits were using these images for more than one reason. This is why multiple-meaning messages can be so significant—and so easily misunderstood.

Additional levels of significance exist in many of the messages I receive. In this case, they were deeply rooted in love and concern by those on the Other Side. Since both of the recipients of these messages were filmmakers, the images didn't frighten them. Instead, bats and wolves allowed the clients to know that the spirits were fully aware of what was going on in their lives. The loved ones may have physically died, but they still knew what was going on in the material world. This was comforting and healing for both of my clients.

A PERSON WHO has transitioned to the Other Side continues to care about those remaining in the material world. Multiple-meaning messages are a dynamic, colorful, and sometimes humorous way for spirits to express that love and concern.

During a reading for Sharlene, the spirit of her son, Hugh, came through.

"He appears young—like in his early twenties," I described.

"Hugh was twenty-three when he died." Sharlene expressed her sadness.

"I'm getting that this was a quick and unexpected passing... I'm feeling a dizzy sensation, which indicates an impaired state of mind, like maybe he was under the influence of drugs. Somehow, this seems coupled with a warmth flowing through me...and this warmth isn't good like a warm and happy feeling. It's traveling through me as if it were injected." I shared what Hugh's spirit seemed to be conveying.

"My son died of a drug overdose," Sharlene acknowledged softly.

"It appears to have been opiates. That would account for the warm sensation," I explained. My years of experience as a criminal defense attorney have brought me many clients who were addicted to heroin and morphine. They've told me that shooting up creates a warm, comfortably numb sensation at first.

"It was heroin," Sharlene confirmed.

"Now he is referencing another son—his brother here in the material world," I relayed.

"Yes, that's my other son, Tyler. He's had a difficult time coping with Hugh's death."

"Hugh indicates Tyler is very nervous, almost to the point of panic attacks. Is that true?" I asked.

"Absolutely," Sharlene replied.

"I am learning that there is a tremendously creative side to this young man," I continued.

Sharlene nodded. "Tyler is very creative and artistic."

"He has a great need for validation—and to express himself," I explained.

"Yes, that's true. Tyler has always needed validation."

"Hugh says to let Tyler know how much you love him, but don't smother him or be too controlling," I conveyed.

"Well, I am a mom." Sharlene chuckled.

Then I paused, not knowing exactly how to convey the next piece of evidence. I'm a firm believer that I must give what I get and not filter information I receive from a spirit. However, I try to be diplomatic and sensitive to my clients.

"Hugh is describing Tyler as shy with girls."

Sharlene laughed. "He's gay, but it's okay. I truly love and accept my son."

"Super!" I said, relieved I didn't have to diplomatically maneuver through the topic. However, the next message gave me pause. "I don't know how to tell you this one—but I know I have to say it."

"I can handle it, Mark." Sharlene wanted to know everything.

"He is saying, tell Tyler to hold out for a nice Mormon boy."

"Oh my gosh!" Sharlene burst into laughter. "That's hilarious! Lots of Mormons live where Tyler and I live, and we see these young Mormon missionaries riding around on their bikes all the time. Tyler admires them."

Intrigued, I listened as Sharlene continued.

"Tyler is always talking about how he wishes he could meet a nice, clean-cut guy like one of those Mormon missionaries," she explained. "This is unbelievable! Tyler doesn't believe in an afterlife or any of this. This will rock his world!"

I felt Hugh wasn't finished yet. It dawned on me that this was a multiple-meaning message. The full impact and depth was still coming to me from Hugh's spirit.

"I'm glad I conveyed what I got—but there is even more to that message, Sharlene. Hugh says Tyler needs a man in his life who doesn't do drugs, has values, won't cheat, and who will take care of him," I explained.

"You can say that again," Sharlene confirmed. "He has always been involved with the worst sort—guys that use him and take advantage of him."

"Hugh also says Tyler needs someone with wholesome values who will give him the care and attention he requires."

"That's uncanny! I can't wait to share all this with Tyler!" Sharlene laughed.

"Hugh is worried about his brother's lack of respect for himself and the way he allows others, particularly the men he gets involved with, to abuse him," I conveyed.

Sharlene's laughter faded. "Hugh is right."

"Hugh knows that Tyler feels alone and isolated, and he wants to applaud Tyler for pushing forward with his life in a more positive way."

"Tyler has been heading down the wrong path for years," Sharlene explained. "He got involved in a string of empty relationships with men who encouraged him to drink and do drugs, and he contracted HIV as a result."

"From what Hugh says, it looks like Tyler is pulling himself out of a rut," I shared.

"He is, and it's not been easy on him," Sharlene admitted. "Tyler doesn't believe in mediums. He thinks all this is hogwash. I can't wait to tell him about all this! I'm hoping the news will give him a spiritual awakening; he needs one."

In no way do I want to imply that homosexuality leads to a life of drugs and loneliness. That antiquated thinking has its basis in prejudice and ignorance. This multiple-meaning message was specific to Tyler. Additionally, Hugh's spirit applauded Tyler for taking control of his life and working to emerge from his difficulties. Further, the account of this reading is in no way meant to reflect in any negative way on the Church of Jesus Christ of Latter Day Saints or upon the young men of faith who serve as its missionaries.

The communication during the reading merely presented specific cultural references to which Sharlene and Tyler could relate. If this reading had been conducted in Japan, for instance, the spirit might have conveyed an image of a young Buddhist monk as an appropriate match for Tyler. Taken in that cultural context, a Buddhist monk would represent the paragon of virtue. As you can see, multiple-meaning messages are complex and unique to the recipient of the message.

SPIRITS REACH OUT to assist us in many ways. Perhaps their greatest purpose is to help us heal from the pain caused by death. Multiple-meaning messages are often a colorful vehicle for that inspirational healing.

Leonardo da Vinci said, "A painter should begin every canvas with a wash of black, because all things in nature are dark except when exposed by the light." Michelangelo, da Vinci's contemporary and artistic rival, once remarked, "Good painting is nothing else but a copy of the perfections of God and a reminder of God's painting."

Art is an integral part of every culture. Whether it's prehistoric paintings of bulls by cave dwellers or images of American presidents carved into the granite of Mount Rushmore, art carries with it powerful associations, emotions, and meaning on multiple levels. On one level, it may be just a creative means of depicting the finite world surrounding us. On a deeper level, it may be an attempt to perceive the infinity of the world beyond.

"The spirit of a young, muscular man is coming through. Wait a second—I recognize him," I said to Kristy at the beginning of a reading.

"What do you mean?" Kristy asked.

"In my experience, a spirit is as eager to communicate with a loved one here as the loved one is with the spirit," I explained. "It's not unusual for a spirit to show up around me prior to the reading."

"Who is it?" Kristy wanted to know.

"I've felt the presence of a male spirit around me all day. I meditate prior to readings, and during my meditation today, he made his presence even clearer. He's a big, muscular tough guy, and he is saying, 'Hi, Mom.'"

"My son was very muscular and strong," Kristy responded.

"His passing was sudden—a sudden impact. It was very fast. In a split second, he was standing there looking down at his body, and then he realized he was outside his body," I described. "It seems like a vehicle accident."

"Yes, he died in a motorcycle crash," she said flatly.

"I realize no mother ever wants to hear things like this, but he is insistent and wants you to know that the separation from his body felt 'cool.'"

"He would," Kristy confirmed, sitting up straight in her chair.

"I see a helmet and the colors red and white...do you recognize their significance?"

"Well, he was wearing a red helmet, and his motorcycle had white stripes," she replied.

"Your son was a tough guy—big, strong. Now I'm seeing a red flag with some gold lettering. It looks like the Marine Corps flag."

"He was a marine." Kristy smiled. "I was so proud of him."

"Your son says, 'A real man never hits a woman,'" I conveyed. "Now he's projecting an image. I see him holding a kitten…does that make any sense to you?"

"He was very gentle with animals, women, and children. The last picture I have of him is a video I took in which he is holding and petting a small kitten in a pet store," Kristy said softly.

"There's an older gentleman with him, someone called Pop or something like that," I described.

"His grandfather on his father's side was called Poppa," Kristy responded.

"He's laughing with his grandfather. Your son says things are cool between the two of them, and he wants you to know he is not alone. They're having a good time, and he's happy," I relayed.

Kristy interrupted, "I have a question, Mark."

"Go ahead."

"Is he disappointed his life was cut so short?"

I conveyed the message I received. "What you call life, I call eternity." Kristy didn't respond.

"I'm seeing an image of what I perceive to be Jesus carrying the cross. It was Simon who offered to carry the cross for Jesus. Your son says, 'If I could have spared you this burden of pain, Mom, I would have.'"

"That's interesting," Kristy commented.

"He says, 'If I could have lived for another twenty-four hours—just another twenty-four hours…' Why is that important?" I wondered aloud.

"I was supposed to see him the next day," Kristy explained.

"Well, he has a message for you." I felt the spirit's vibrational energy increasing.

"Yes?"

"God exists."

Kristy listened as the multiple-meaning message unfolded.

"When he stepped out of his body after the motorcycle crash, your son says, 'There was a warm and loving presence welcoming me to a new life—an eternal life.'"

"Is that the message?" Kristy asked.

"He says, 'God gave me a new birth—a new life,'" I relayed.

Kristy listened quietly, her eyes focused and intense.

"And now I'm seeing something truly amazing," I said as a familiar image appeared in my mind's eye.

"What is it?"

"It's a scene from the Sistine Chapel," I told her.

Kristy was silent.

"It's Michelangelo's *Creation of Adam*—an image of God giving life to Adam."

Kristy remained silent.

"Does this resonate with you?" I could see Kristy trying to maintain her composure.

"It does, Mark. My son's name is Adam."

8

Frequency Beacons:
The Two-Way Street of Love

Prior to an interdimensional communication session, it is natural for someone to be excited over the prospect of making a connection with a loved one in spirit. What many people may not realize is that spirits are just as excited to communicate with us in the material world as we are about receiving messages from them. The common denominator is the two-way street of love. Love transcends physical death and is the binding energetic force between all sentient beings.

This is why, in interdimensional communication, it is the spirits of our loved ones who are the first to communicate because these spirits are closer to us than other spirits. Evidential mediumship is predicated on communication with spirits the client will recognize and be able to verify based on pieces of evidence presented by the medium.

Many people wonder why relatives from centuries ago do not necessarily communicate. As thrilling as it might be to communicate with Mary Todd Lincoln or King Henry VIII, intimate details about those who died long ago cannot necessarily be verified by the person receiving the messages. The more distant the emotional tie, the less likely a spirit will be motivated to communicate with someone here. It's not that the spirit can't—it's more a matter of whether a spirit wants to. The vast majority of the time, interdimensional communication is centered on the personal connection between the spirit and the person here. Free will isn't just a material world commodity; it also exists on the Other Side.

Those of us in the material world are limited when we try to comprehend infinity through the lens of the finite. Despite its finite nature, the following explanation may help illustrate how spirits remain connected to us—and how they know when to contact us.

From an energy standpoint, we are all connected to people here in the material world as well as to spirits on the Other Side. So even though a loved one has passed, you are still energetically linked. When released from the finite confines of a physical body, spirits are pure energetic consciousness. There is nothing idle about the Other Side. Spirits don't get tired or require sleep; this means they are always active. They're always learning, striving to ascend to higher levels on the Other Side, and performing responsibilities we cannot even begin to comprehend. This includes an awareness of what is happening with a loved one in the material world.

Now, visualize being tethered to everyone you know and have ever known. Imagine these tethered connections as strands in a vast three-dimensional spider web (minus the spider, of course). This web stretches in all directions. Each tether of this web is an energy beam. These beams extend far beyond the people you know to every living being.

However, let's keep this example closer to home and just focus on the energetic connections with loved ones who've passed. When you miss a deceased loved one and grieve, this expends a lot of energy. Everyone who has experienced death understands how exhausting the grieving process is. This energy buildup caused by the emotional intensity emits a frequency beacon, which vibrates along this energy beam connected to a loved one in spirit. It's a lot like the vibration along a spider web when something is caught. Similarly, the frequency beacon notifies the spirit that energy is being directed at him or her.

Frequency beacons are emitted in many different circumstances, such as missing a deceased loved one immensely, thinking about that person, saying something aloud to that person, sharing a memory about that person, or just expressing a feeling of love for that person. The energy of these emotions creates the vibrational frequency beacon that attracts the spirit's attention to you.

Interdimensional communication is a two-way street. On the flip side of the cosmic coin, sometimes a spirit wants to contact you. A spirit can send you frequency beacons, which actually are signs from the Other Side. The energetic vibration of these frequency beacons can direct attention to the spirit's presence in many ways. We might experience a visitation while in the dream state or have a feeling that the spirit's presence is near—or hear the spirit's voice, catch a glimpse of that person's energy in our peripheral vision, or smell a familiar scent associated with the person. Frequency beacons can motivate us to perform a physical act such as switching on a radio to hear a special song that reminds us of our loved one. The frequency beacon can even direct our attention to objects. Imagine finding a penny every time you thought about someone on the Other Side—literally, pennies from heaven!

Since spirits are aware of what is happening in our lives, they also know when there will be a direct conduit for communication, meaning a medium, in close proximity to a loved one they want to contact. The spirit may decide to send a frequency beacon to the medium.

While on tour promoting *Never Letting Go*, I was invited by Jean Haller, owner of Journeys of Life Bookstore in Pittsburgh, to conduct a book signing and gallery readings. As my tour manager, Rocky, and I drove through the bucolic hills of

West Virginia on the way to Pittsburgh, I found myself humming and then singing the "Yo Ho (A Pirate's Life for Me)" song from Walt Disney World's *Pirates of the Caribbean* ride.

"Mark! If you're that desperate for music, turn on the radio," Rocky complained.

"Huh?"

"You've been singing that *Pirates of the Caribbean* song for the last ten miles! Could you give it a rest?" she asked.

"Well, matey! Shiver me timbers! Arrgh!" I joked.

"Keep it up and I'm going to make you walk the plank!" Rocky chuckled as she handed me a bottle of water, most likely to keep me from singing.

Then I realized what was happening. The logical portion of my brain had been engaged in driving, allowing the emotional side of my brain to wander into the daydream state of alpha wave production, which occurs during spirit communication.

"It's a spirit! I know when a spirit is trying to get a message through. He's coming in a bit clearer now. I am seeing a red sports car—like a Corvette…" I described.

"So that's it!" Rocky exclaimed. "I've seen this happen to you before. Spirits come to you before the reading sometimes, don't they?"

"Yeah, they do. This guy also feels grandfatherly, and he's very persistent." I banged my fist on the steering wheel.

"Uh, Mark, would you please not do this when you're driving?" Rocky urged.

"I can't get that song out of my head," I said as I started humming the melody.

"Mark!" Rocky interrupted. "Stop! You're doing it again!"

Rocky switched on a radio news program. The song receded from my mind.

After we had settled into our hotel in Pittsburgh, Rocky and I met with Jean Haller at Journeys of Life Bookstore. I always pray and meditate prior to conducting readings. I pray the rosary and ask God to send forth spirits for the highest of purposes to bring messages of love, healing, and resolution. Meanwhile, the *Pirates of the Caribbean* song returned and continued to fill my head. I looked forward to connecting this spirit with a loved one who most likely would be waiting in the audience.

The gallery readings that evening went well. Many in the audience received messages conveyed through me by their loved ones. About halfway through my presentation, I started hearing that same song again. I suddenly found myself singing the pirate song.

The gallery audience became absolutely silent. Everyone stared at me. Somehow I felt like I'd just been sentenced to walk the plank. I stopped singing long enough to ask, "Does that song mean anything to anyone here?"

No one responded.

I continued, "I've had a man's spirit around me all day—he feels like a grandfather—and I keep hearing this song from *Pirates of the Caribbean*. Does that movie or a trip to Disney World resonate with anyone here?"

Once again, no response.

"What about a red sports car—a candy-apple red Corvette?"

Nothing. Complete silence.

"This is really strong. A grandfather…he's singing the *Pirates of the Caribbean* song—Disney World—red Corvette… *anyone?*"

The audience continued to stare at me. The looks on their faces told me that none of it meant a thing to anyone there. If there had been a plank nearby, I would've taken my chances on it.

Gallery readings can be a wonderful means of connecting a few people in attendance with their loved ones in spirit. To me, such an event is more challenging than trying a court case—yet so much more rewarding. Gallery readings, though, are not without problems, and this night I was having a big one, so I asked that spirit to step aside. When he did so, I was able to carry on and connect a married couple with the spirit of their daughter.

When the event was over and the audience had departed, Rocky talked to Jean as I gathered my things.

"Excuse me, Mr. Anthony," I heard someone say. I looked up to see the young woman employed as the store's sales clerk.

"Yes, can I help you?" I asked.

"Hi, yeah…my name is Penny…and, like, the man with the red Corvette? That was my grandfather," she said.

Rocky and Jean stopped in mid-sentence and looked toward Penny and me.

"Are you sure?" Her comment took me completely by surprise.

"Totally! I really liked the *Pirates of the Caribbean* movie, and my grandfather promised to take me to Disney World just so, like, we could go on that ride," she explained.

"Okay," I said, confused as to why she hadn't spoken up earlier.

"But, like, he died right before we were supposed to go to Disney World...and my grandmother had bad financial problems and she, like, wants to sell his vintage candy-apple red Corvette but doesn't know if she should. And it's still in the garage, covered up exactly like Grandpa left it."

"Why didn't you say something during the gallery reading?" I asked.

"I didn't want to look stupid," she replied.

So it's better if I look stupid? I thought, remembering the audience's awkward silence. But then I realized she was just a shy teenager.

"Penny, your grandfather has been with me all day, driving me nuts with that song," I told her gently.

"I'm sorry if I made you look bad," she said mournfully. "I just didn't know what to do."

"Penny! Next time, raise your hand! Please don't be afraid to speak up if you know the message is for you. You could've missed something really important."

"My grandmother is about to lose her house. Selling Grandpa's car will let her keep it," Penny revealed. "Grandma is so sad—she hates the idea of selling something that meant so much to him."

Pirates of the Caribbean cranked up loudly in my head again. Apparently Grandpa was back. Penny listened carefully as I conveyed, "He's well aware of that, and he wants to make sure you tell your grandmother to sell the car, even though it's painful for her to do so. He says her security is far more important than any car." As soon as I finished speaking, the *Pirates of the Caribbean* song stopped. The spirit let me know I had delivered his message. Mission accomplished.

"Thank you," Penny said meekly. "I think I'll go see Grandma now."

IT IS NOT unusual for people to be reluctant to speak up during a gallery reading. Even though it would have been easy to be frustrated with this young woman, it is important for a medium to always remember that spirit contact isn't about the medium. It is about the person for whom the message is meant. A medium is merely the conduit that delivers it.

If you find yourself in a situation like this during a gallery reading and you know the spirit is there for you, let the medium know. Even though you may initially think you don't need to respond, you may miss significant information like a message of love and resolution or something even more complex like a multiple-meaning message. When a spirit is making the effort to communicate, extend the courtesy of acknowledging the contact.

DURING A LECTURE I conducted in Newington, New Hampshire, a woman asked, "Can dead people see you when you're on the toilet?" Needless to say, the audience and I cracked up with laughter. However, the chuckles soon gave way to concerned looks from the majority of those assembled.

"Well, can they?" another woman asked.

"Yeah, I feel my late wife around me whenever…ya know," a man confirmed.

It is true. Many people sense the presence of a loved one in spirit when they're in the bathroom. This may not be as outlandish as it sounds. It isn't that spirits are more likely to appear when you're in the bathroom; it is that they're more likely to be detected by you.

People tend to sing in the shower…why? It's because they're relaxed and not afraid to express themselves. Certainly, being relaxed and letting your emotional guard down is part of opening up to the frequency and vibration of spirit contact. However, there are technical reasons as well.

Since spirits are energy, the more conducive the environment is to conducting energetic and electrical impulses, the easier it is to sense the presence of spirits. Bathrooms have a lot of hard surfaces—like tile, marble, porcelain, and concrete. One of the reasons people like to sing in the shower is because sound-wave energy resonates more clearly in environs that have hard surfaces. Metal and water are both superb conductors of electricity, and bathrooms are loaded with them. When you're in a bathroom, you are in a highly conductive place—and it becomes easier to pick up the vibrations and frequency beacons emitted by spirits.

Please don't get worried about this. Spirits respect our privacy; having been in human form, they certainly understand bodily functions. They are not intruding. It's just that you happen to be in a better environment for the vibrational energy of frequency beacons. If having spirits around you in the bathroom is an issue, simply ask them to give you privacy. They will want to give you your space.

And this doesn't mean I'm going to start conducting readings in bathrooms, although sometimes I also forget to ask them to respect my privacy. One morning, I was getting ready for work, and while in the shower, I suddenly felt a severe pressure in my chest. I began to get concerned—and then I saw the spirit of a middle-aged man with a dark complexion clutching his chest. This indicated a spirit who had passed from a heart attack.

While I am always respectful to spirits, as far as I was concerned, I felt this wasn't the proper time or place for interdimensional communication, so I said aloud, "Excuse me, sir...a little privacy, please?"

With that, the spirit smiled and receded from my perception. Although he had been rather persistent, he respected my request and I sensed he was a kind and considerate man. Spirits maintain their personality, likes and dislikes, memories, and habits on the Other Side. That is why spirits tend to communicate from the Other Side much in the same way they did while in the material world. Shy and quiet spirits can be challenging in communication; those who were outgoing and boisterous while alive are more forthcoming.

Later that day, when I returned from court to my office, I was scheduled to conduct a reading via the Internet for a woman overseas. When I finished my prayers and meditation, I put on my headset and switched on the computer link.

A beautiful Indian woman's face appeared on my screen. From the way she was dressed, I could see she was a Hindu. Suddenly the spirit of the middle-aged man I'd seen earlier appeared to me again. I described his physical appearance and said, "He looks like he is from India and, to me, it feels like he died of a heart attack."

"Yes, that is my father. We are from India, and he did die of a heart attack."

I was so excited to have this confirmation that I said without thinking, "I recognize him! He was in the shower with me this morning!"

"What?" she exclaimed. "He's been dead for a year! What are you saying about my father?"

"No, no! I mean," I said, unable to suppress my laughter, "I saw his spirit this morning when I was getting ready for work. It's easier to perceive spirits in the bathroom because of the conductivity—all the tile, metal, and water make a stronger energetic connection."

"You are right! This is indeed very funny," she giggled. "And it makes perfect sense—I'm a television producer here in India, and I understand completely the intricacies of wireless signals and transmissions."

"Spirits are energy, and he knew you were going to be talking to me today so he wanted to make sure I'd recognize him," I explained.

"Father was very funny. I miss his sense of humor. He was also very punctual and insisted on always arriving early for appointments."

"Isn't it comforting to know some things never change?" I reassured her.

ALTHOUGH SPIRITS LIKE to let us know they are aware of what is going on in our lives, frequency beacons are a two-way street. Evidential mediumship requires that the medium convey pieces of information communicated by a spirit that can then be verified by the client. This requires the client to listen to what is presented and then let the medium know whether the information presented is accurate. Spirits are never wrong; what *can* be wrong is the interpretation by the medium or the client's understanding of the message.

During a reading for Misty, the spirit of her great-grandfather kept showing me the image of a large birthday cake.

"I'm seeing a big birthday cake. This indicates that someone close to you just had a birthday or is about to have a birthday," I conveyed.

"Hmmm, can't think of anyone," Misty replied.

"So, no one close to you had a birthday recently?"

"Nope!" Misty seemed sure of her information.

"Is someone's birthday coming up?"

"No, I don't think so."

"Are you sure it's not your great-grandfather's birthday?"

"No, that isn't for months," she answered.

"This is really strong! Could it be someone connected to your great-grandfather?"

"But Mark, it's not his birthday—that was three months ago," she told me.

"It really seems important because your great-grandfather's spirit keeps showing me this huge birthday cake with lots of candles on it. You are somehow connected to this celebration."

"Oh, wait! I almost forgot! Earlier today I was at my great-grandmother's one-hundredth birthday party. She's my great-grandfather's wife—do you think that's what he could be talking about?"

It is not unusual during a reading for people to not immediately recognize the information being transmitted. My experience has shown me that many people are overwhelmed by the information or nervous during the reading. They simply need time to process the information in order to receive the maximum benefit from the reading.

Many pieces of evidence that come through during interdimensional communication may not make sense to the client right away. The client may be overwhelmed emotionally and by the volume of messages and information that he or she does not immediately understand. It often requires a period of reflection after the reading, which can take hours, days, or even longer to fully understand what was conveyed.

This is also why it is a good idea to take notes or record the session.

WHEN A GROUP of people who have deceased loved ones in common gather, this mass energetic emission of love sends out quite a powerful barrage of frequency beacons. It appears the intensity of these energy beacons is increased when the group gathers for the express purpose of engaging in interdimensional communication.

During the Women's Expo in Toms River, New Jersey, I gave a presentation about "Intuition: The Key to Your Success." The audience was extremely receptive. After my talk, I was invited to one of the attendee's homes on the following day to conduct a group reading. My tour manager, Rocky, and I had been on a long tour of New York and New Jersey, and we both found it soothing to drive along the scenic New Jersey shore and smell the ocean air again.

Our host, Denise, had a beautiful home on the water in Toms River. Denise and her aunts Diane, Joanie, and Barbara, as well as her sister-in-law Monica, greeted us. Denise's husband, Steve, an open-minded skeptic, was curious and decided to observe the reading. This was a happy, enthusiastic, talkative, and loving family. Rocky nicknamed these women the Jersey Gals.

The reading took place in a large living room with French doors overlooking the river. Most of the Jersey Gals were seated on a long, comfortable leather sofa. Rocky sat in an armchair off to their right so she could take notes. Steve and Monica sat in matching armchairs to their left. I borrowed a chair from the kitchen and set it in front of a cozy fireplace so I could face everyone. Steve's chocolate Labrador retriever curled up on the floor next to me for a snooze. It was a warm and welcoming environment.

Prior to every reading, I give a short orientation to explain how I perceive information. This is to clarify what certain feelings and sensations can mean to me and how they can be interpreted so the clients will receive the maximum benefit from the interdimensional communication. The more the clients understand about the process, the more likely the messages will make sense to them.

"Spirits communicate from the Other Side very much like they did when they were here in the material world," I started. "If someone was shy and quiet when they were alive, that spirit can be challenging. However, if they were gregarious and outgoing—"

"You mean like Jersey spirits!" Diane interrupted jokingly. Everyone in the room cracked up.

"Yeah," I chuckled, catching the mood. "Those Jersey spirits are usually very forthcoming!"

"I don't think you'll have a problem with our spirits being shy," Joanie added.

"Okay, Jersey Gals, Steve, and spirits…this is going to be a bit of a workout!" I said as I sensed more than a dozen spirits adjusting their frequencies so I could perceive them.

"Monica, a woman on the grandmother level is coming through for you," I relayed.

"Super! Do you know which grandmother?" Monica asked enthusiastically.

"Something about a cuckoo clock…I know that may sound cuckoo, but I give what I get, and there's a connection between the grandmother and a cuckoo clock," I told her.

"Oh my gosh! My grandmother on my mother's side of the family was from Germany, and she gave me a cuckoo clock. I've never taken it out of the box," Monica confessed.

"Your grandmother says it's time to put the cuckoo clock up on the wall," I conveyed.

"Will do!" she replied cheerfully.

"I'm being drawn to Denise…" I started. Everyone in the room became very attentive.

"There is a male—he is on your generational level, which means a brother, cousin, friend, or spouse. His death feels like a sudden and unexpected passing. I'm feeling a massive pain in my chest, like he might have died of a heart attack. He was in motion, and then *wham!* It feels like he collapsed." I waited for a response from Denise.

"That's my husband, Charlie. He died of a heart attack when he was jogging," Denise explained.

"I'm being directed by this spirit to Steve," I told her.

Steve's eyebrows rose. Obviously, he wasn't expecting this.

"He—Charlie, that is—wants to thank you, Steve, for being such a good friend. You spent a lot of time together.

Charlie is acknowledging the two of you talked to each other a lot."

Steve nodded. "Yeah, he was my best friend. We talked every day. As a matter of fact, we were on the phone to each other constantly. We actually spoke on the phone a couple hours before he died; we were planning a fishing trip."

"Charlie wants to thank you for taking care of Denise. He is saying, 'Please don't hold it against the kids; they need time,'" I relayed.

Denise interjected, "My children just can't accept the fact that I married Steve. They are angry at me for marrying him."

The next message made me smile. "Charlie says, 'It's okay; besides, Steve, you're not as good as I am!' I get the impression he's making some sort of inside joke, Steve."

"That's Charlie's sense of humor!" Denise explained.

"He's very upbeat and keeps joking that he's okay with everything, but he's still the best," I conveyed.

"Charlie was a very competitive guy. He always beat me in every sport we played together. That last message helps me because now I know for sure that he's okay with Denise and me getting married." Steve seemed relieved. He turned to Denise and met her eyes, smiling gently.

"Another man is coming through now. It feels like he's been on the Other Side a long time—looks like he's from the '50s," I described.

"That could be a lot of people!" Joanie acknowledged, a twinkle in her eye.

"He's thin, athletic, has kind of a V-shaped build…strong but not real muscular. He reminds me of that actor Sal Mineo," I explained. "You know, it's not unusual for me to get images of actors or clips from TV or films to help me describe the appearance or personality of a spirit."

The room became very quiet. Barbara leaned forward. Her sisters, Diane and Joanie, shot each other concerned glances.

"I feel my lungs filling up with fluid; there's water all around—water is rushing in!" I found it hard to speak. "He fought it—he fought it! And then he was pulled under…it didn't last long, and everything went black."

A tear rolled down Barbara's cheek. "Oh my god!" she exclaimed. "That has to be Johnny."

"He was Barbara's husband—he drowned," Joanie added.

"He says the two of you weren't together very long," I continued, looking at Barbara.

"No, they weren't. They had just gotten married…" Diane said.

"He's been on the Other Side a long time," I reiterated.

"The two of them were at the shore together on Labor Day weekend in 1959," Joanie clarified.

"A little boy was swimming and got caught in a rip tide." Denise picked up the story.

"The kid's father was trying to swim to his son, but he couldn't," Joanie added.

"Or he wouldn't because he wasn't a strong swimmer, but my Johnny—he was a fireman," Barbara took over the conversation. "Johnny didn't even think twice about his own safety. He jumped right in and swam to rescue that little boy."

"He was able to get to the kid and throw him over a wave to his father and saved his life," Diane added.

"Johnny rescued the boy, but then the rip tide pulled him under, and he disappeared beneath the waves. Suddenly, he was gone!" Decades of mourning flooded Barbara's soft eyes. She'd carried this pain for a long time.

Diane sighed. "His body washed up on the shore three days later."

"And the family of that boy never even said thank you," Joanie remembered.

Barbara said quietly, "They didn't even come to Johnny's funeral…"

"There's more," I said, focusing my attention back to Johnny's spirit. "Johnny wants you to know he went into the Light. It is bright and peaceful and happy where he is! Johnny was there to greet a father figure whose name sounds like Larry."

"Larry!" the Jersey Gals shouted in unison.

"That's our father!" Diane exclaimed.

"Johnny was there to greet your dad, Larry, when he crossed into the Light. Well, there were a lot of people there to greet Larry, and I feel that some of them will be making contact during this reading." I was receiving a sense of more activity.

Larry's appearance brightened the mood in the room.

"Now, Larry is talking about a gold coin. It looks to be about the size of one of those old five-dollar gold pieces," I conveyed. "Does that make sense? Is there a connection between Larry and gold coins?"

"No, I can't place it. Anyone?" Diane asked. No one else seemed able to make a connection.

"That's okay." I explained, "It's not unusual for some things that come up during readings to not make sense right away. Let's move on to the next message." The group session continued as spirits reached from across heaven's veil to make contact with those they loved here in the material world.

The next day, Rocky and I headed to the Newark airport. I was driving when Rocky's cell phone rang. It was a call from the Jersey Gals.

"Mark! You have to hear this!" Rocky said, switching on the speaker function of her phone.

"You won't believe what happened after you left!" Barbara exclaimed.

"Last night during the reading, our father, Larry, came through, and you said there was some connection between him and a gold coin," Diane said.

"I remember," I replied, intrigued. "Tell me more."

"I drove Barbara to her house, parked, and we walked up to the front door," Diane explained.

"And?"

"Right in front of her door—right on the threshold of her front door—oh my god!" Diane exclaimed.

"Right in front of the door—what?" I asked. Now I *really* wanted to know.

"There was a gold coin!" the Jersey Gals said all together.

"And here's the best part," Barbara added. "It wasn't gold—but it was gold colored."

"How's that the best part?" I wondered.

"It was a commemorative coin, and it had the image of an angel engraved on it. And the inscription on the coin read 'angel in my pocket,'" Barbara explained.

"It had to be Daddy!" Barbara practically yelled into the phone.

"And this is the weird part," Diane explained. "No one knows how it got there. No one had anything like that coin, and it definitely wasn't there when we left to go to Denise's house for the reading."

"It's a sign from Daddy—that he's in heaven with my Johnny and they're both watching over us," Barbara added.

Spirit contact doesn't have an expiration date. Even if someone has been on the Other Side for what we consider a long time—like Barbara's husband, Johnny—the spirit is perfectly capable of responding to a frequency beacon. However, spirits aren't on our timetable. Since the Other Side is timeless, this can be frustrating to people in the material world. Grief-stricken people often want answers right away and wonder why prayers to God and questions for spirits are not immediately answered. Nonetheless, God is always listening.

ALICE AND STUART traveled from Wisconsin to Florida for a reading with me. They were a warm, gracious, down-to-earth couple—the very epitome of Midwestern sensibility. If there are such things as soul mates, then these two people had to be that. Although they'd been married for over forty years, Alice and Stuart seemed more like newlyweds, head over heels in love.

"January in Florida certainly is a lot different than January in Wisconsin," Stuart remarked, shaking my hand.

"What a lovely sunny day!" Alice said cheerfully as they both took their seats.

At the beginning of each session, I say a prayer because prayer raises vibrational frequency. As soon as I said amen at the end of the prayer, a presence came forth.

"This is a male spirit, he feels young—like a son," I indicated.

"That's our son, Terry," Stuart confided somberly.

"We were hoping to hear from him," Alice added.

"May—I'm hearing an M word that starts with *may*," I conveyed.

"Doesn't ring a bell." Alice shook her head.

"Does the month of May have any significance?"

"Not that I can think of," Stuart answered after a pause.

Alice added, "I can't think of anything about May that relates to our son."

But the sound *may* kept resonating through me. "Let me stick with this for a bit—it's really important," I explained, closing my eyes and taking a deep breath.

"May—Mable—maple!" I recited. "It's maple. I'm seeing a single maple leaf, so this message has something to do with a maple tree or a maple leaf—and this feels significant."

"I can't imagine what that could be." Alice's face expressed her confusion.

"It was so cold that day—so cold! I'm seeing images of ice, frost, and snow," I continued. "This has to do with the maple leaf."

"I don't remember if there was a maple tree near our house," Alice said, looking more perplexed.

"No, it's not that!" Stuart interjected.

Alice and I looked at each other. Stuart took a deep breath and continued, "There wasn't a maple tree for miles—but I do know what this means."

"You do?" Alice asked.

"It's a secret I've never told anyone—not even you." Stuart's eyes reddened. Maintaining his composure, he reached deep into his heart to bring forth the explanation. Even though his son had died ten years earlier, I could see that the pain was still a gaping wound.

"It was so cold the day of Terry's funeral; January in Wisconsin usually is. After the service we went back to the house," Stuart remembered. "I stood alone in front of our house. It was so still: no breeze, no movement of air. I asked Terry to give me a sign—anything—to let me know he was somehow still connected to me."

Alice listened pensively.

"Suddenly a single maple leaf…it just descended—floated, actually—straight down to the ground," he recalled.

Alice and I sat still, transfixed.

"There wasn't a maple tree for miles. The strangest thing was that this was in the dead of winter. It was January, and the leaves had all fallen a couple months earlier, but this particular leaf looked fresh—like it had just turned a golden yellow."

Stuart paused and took a deep breath.

"I looked at this one maple leaf sitting at the edge of the driveway and I thought *now that's interesting*," Stuart confided. "But I'm a bit skeptical, so I said out loud, 'If you're my son or from my son, make the leaf move!'"

Alice gazed intently at Stuart.

"And then the darnedest thing happened. The leaf began to flutter—and, mind you, there wasn't even a hint of a breeze. It was totally still. This maple leaf begins fluttering and almost walking! It flutters right up to me—right up the driveway—and lands at my feet!"

"Why didn't you tell me?" Alice asked softly. "You kept it a secret all these years?"

"I did because I didn't know what to think. I just didn't know if it was real," Stuart said.

"Our boy died ten years ago this week," Alice said, gently taking Stuart's hand.

"Alice, for ten years I've been looking for the answer—some confirmation that it really was a sign from our son. And now I believe it was."

9

Consciousness and Personality
Are Eternal

The great religions of the world agree that we are more than just a physical body. They teach that the spirit, also known as the soul, preexists the body and lives on in an eternal state after the body ceases to function. Since the 1970s, survival of consciousness studies conducted by the scientific community have been producing evidence in support of this belief.

Despite the power of faith and the evidence of science, it is easy to feel the sum total of the self is the physical body. This is because we are born, we grow old, and then we die, yet we are so much more than a physical container. People are spirits having a brief material world existence. The body may be finite, but the spirit is infinite.

Consciousness is the awareness and intelligence enshrined within a spirit. It contains the attributes that give a person his or her uniqueness. These include personality, observations, experiences, knowledge, and love for others. The attributes of a spirit are eternal and live on even after physical death.

Consciousness also encompasses an awareness of the self and interaction of the self with the material world dimension and the dimensions of the Other Side. It is a perception of things beyond the scope of our five physical senses of sight, hearing, smell, taste, and touch. However, awareness of the existence of something does not necessarily mean full comprehension of it. For example, every day we switch on electric lights. Although we may be aware of electricity, how many of us truly understand how it actually works?

Similarly, an awareness of infinity does not mean that those of us living in the material world can begin to comprehend it. Our brain is designed to process only finite concepts. This is because everything we experience in the material world has limits and boundaries—a beginning and an end. However, once beyond the confines of a finite body, the infinite spirit is perfectly capable of comprehending infinity because the spirit has returned to his or her natural, infinite state of existence.

This is where the brain comes into play. The brain regulates and controls the physical bodily functions and activities. It receives and interprets sensory impulses and stimuli. It also transmits signals to the muscles and organs in the body. The brain is an organ, albeit an extremely sophisticated one, so the question arises: is your brain really you?

The scientific community has traditionally viewed consciousness as a byproduct of brain processes, which means consciousness is generated by the brain. However, pioneers like the late Nobel Laureate and neurobiologist Sir John Eccles, and more recently Dr. Larry Dossey, support the theory that the brain does not create consciousness; it merely houses the consciousness. It also appears the brain does more than just house the consciousness; it seems to be a filter between our material world existence and our connection to the infinity of the Other Side. The brain gives us the ability to function in a finite state. In a sense, it is the arbiter between the finite and the infinite.

Our true self is not generated by the brain. Rather, our true self is a spirit, which is an infinite energetic consciousness. Since our true self is pure energy, we are all linked not only to our loved ones but also to the energy of all life. Energy is neither created nor destroyed; it is only transferred from one form to another. While in pure spiritual form, the energy that makes us who we are never tires, becomes ill, or is prone to the restraints, sadness, and difficulties associated with living in the material world.

Part of a spirit's mission is to evolve through learning and growth. Some of this growth comes from the love, pain, and physical experiences of the material world, which is why spirits incarnate into human form.

Think of your body as a bottle and your brain as the cork in the bottle. We are temporarily in the bottle, but we are not the bottle. Consciousness is created by the spirit, so it is literally bottled up within the body, with the brain acting as the cork to keep the consciousness connected to the finite material world. When the spirit is released from the bottle of the body, the consciousness of the person continues on into eternity in a pure energetic form.

At physical death, the body and the brain cease to function. When the body dies, the physical suffering and ailments of a person end. When the brain dies, the egocentric portions cease to exist. This includes the negativity of anger, fear, hatred, emotional suffering, and mental illness. The consciousness remembers and reflects upon these things, but they are no longer attributes of the consciousness. They are memories of behavior in the material world to be resolved and reconciled.

What this means is that the personality of a person continues after physical death. When the spirit separates from the body, the uniqueness of the person is contained within the spirit—the proverbial drop of water that returns to the ocean of infinity. The unique personality of the spirit remains intact within the individual consciousness and is able to disconnect from the collective consciousness of the Other Side for many reasons. One of those reasons is to resolve issues with people in the material world.

Love, especially between family members, at its purest is unconditional. This means that someone you are raised by or with loves you no matter what. However, that isn't always the case. For many people, the most difficult relationships of all are the ones that are supposed to be the easiest.

CANDICE CONTACTED ME for a telephone reading. I explained as I generally do, prior to our reading, that during interdimensional communication I sometimes see images of actors and even clips from TV shows or movies in my mind's eye. This is a cultural reference that allows me to describe a spirit's physical characteristic or a personality trait.

"Two spirits, a male and a female, are coming through," I described to Candice. "They're both on the parent level."

"Wonderful! I was hoping to hear from my parents!" Candice exclaimed.

"Your parents are very classy. They seem like sophisticated people—glamorous, almost like movie stars."

"My parents weren't movie stars, but they were very glamorous—always the center of attention and talk of the town. They hosted lots of extravagant parties," Candice volunteered.

"Your father reminds me of the actor Cary Grant. I'm told that you always made him so happy. He loved you and still loves you very much."

"Daddy was very suave and handsome like Cary Grant. It is true we were very close," Candice admitted.

"Your mother is coming forward and she reminds me of—uh—oh boy!" I hesitated as an image of a famous actress formed in my mind's eye.

"Who does she remind you of?" Candice asked pointedly.

"Joan Crawford!"

"My mother was *exactly* like Joan Crawford! She even beat me with a wire hanger when I was a little girl," Candice noted bitterly.

"Oh, so this is a reference to the *Mommie Dearest* Joan Crawford," I said recalling the movie I'd seen years before about Crawford. One of the most intense scenes in the movie is where she beat her young daughter with a wire hanger.

"Yes, my mother was quite the socialite. Hollywood glamour on the outside—and a mean bitch behind closed doors. That's her, all right," Candice acknowledged.

"Now your mother is projecting an image of you as Snow White and herself as the Evil Queen. You know, the one who was jealous because Snow White was the fairest of them all," I continued.

"I understand the part about Joan Crawford, but what do you think the Snow White reference means?" Candice asked.

"Your mother was jealous of you," I said as a multiple-meaning message unfolded.

"Jealous of me? Why on earth…?"

"Your mother says she was jealous of your beauty and jealous of your relationship with your father. She resented the fact that she wasn't the only one in the world for your father, and she took it out on you, just like the Evil Queen sought vengeance upon Snow White," I conveyed.

"Really?"

"And there's more, Candice…it isn't exactly an apology, it's more of an explanation. Your mother says 'I didn't kill you, I did my job…and you've done a much better job with your life than I ever did with mine,'" I relayed.

A few days after the reading, I received an email from Candice:

As you saw during the reading, I have been struggling with my feelings of anger, fear, and grief over my relationship with my mother, "Joan Crawford," for my whole life, with no seeming ability to resolve these issues.

I thought I needed an apology from her to feel better. What I found I really needed was an understanding of her feelings and personality. When you said she was "jealous" of the relationship I had with my father, I felt so much compassion in my heart for her.

The analogy to Snow White and the jealous Queen is apt. Although she was skillful at making the most of her looks, my mother had to work at it, and I was naturally a very pretty girl. My father always said all he ever wanted was a beautiful daughter. So the seeds of jealousy were sown. Interesting how what we think of as a fairy tale is such a deeply rooted psychological message.

Strange to think she made me stronger by terrorizing me. On second thought, it does make sense. Both my husband and I are longtime recovering alcoholics and dedicated to sponsoring others in AA who want to take the twelve steps to obtain alcohol recovery and, more importantly, emotional sobriety. I do believe that everything I have experienced, especially in coping with her abuse, has been necessary for me to be able to do what I do now.

I am amazed I came out of the reading with compassion for her after so many years of resentment and sorrow. I also sense Mother is different now, somehow softer. Still tough, but now she's approachable, as if she's evolved into a more loving spirit.

JUST AS A personality survives physical death, so does a spirit's awareness of what is happening in the lives of those they love. Jolene had a complicated family history. She was left with her maternal grandparents when she was an infant. They were loving and kind people who raised her as a daughter. Her grandmother was the person she wanted to speak to the most.

At the beginning of the interdimensional communication, I saw the image of an elderly woman. When I perceive visual images, oftentimes I am made aware of what the spirit appears to be wearing. While it is doubtful spirits need to wear clothing, it is an indication to me of either their occupation or health status prior to death.

"She's depicted in a bathrobe, indicating she was ill quite some time prior to passing. This means she was bedridden or in a hospital," I explained.

"That's true," Jolene confirmed.

"I see her blinking. When I see someone blinking, this means she was having difficulty with lucidity. She was struggling to maintain her mental clarity. This indicates either dementia or treatment with pain medication prior to death."

"Gramma was very ill and heavily medicated, so that makes sense," Jolene responded.

"What about her eyesight? It appears she was having issues there, too. I know lots of elderly people wear glasses, but her glasses seem to be bifocals with particularly thick lenses."

"That's right! She did have really thick glasses. They were bifocals," Jolene recalled.

Before I could continue, Jolene interjected, "Can I ask a question?"

"Go ahead."

"Some things have happened around the house, and I want to know if they could have been a sign from Gramma."

Every medium gets these types of questions. In a way it is to test the psychic, but in another way I find it fascinating. Spirits don't always answer questions, but sometimes they will. So I sat silently and waited for a reply.

"I'm seeing a ceiling fan. It looks brown, although it may also be white," I said, describing the vision.

"Cool!" Jolene replied. "Our two ceiling fans have been going on and off by themselves. And one is brown and the other is white."

While I was excited to know that Gramma answered Jolene's question, I felt there was more to the message.

"There are two reasons she's doing the bit with the fans. One is to let you know she's around, and the other has to do with the wiring in the house."

"Really?" Jolene appeared surprised.

"Gramma is now showing me a fuse box. It looks like it's in what could be a garage," I explained.

"Actually, it's in the basement," Jolene corrected.

"Okay, I live in Florida—we don't have basements, but if we did, that's probably what it would look like," I explained. "The wiring looks old and it's not in good shape, but let me explain. I'm not suggesting you're going to have a fire, but it feels to me like Gramma wants you to have an electrician check it out. There is an issue, but I repeat: you are not in imminent danger."

It is important for the medium not to make an assumption about an image or a message in the absence of substantial evidence. It is also unethical to frighten people. There are enough superstitious people in the world who view interdimensional communication as something negative. The cure for this ignorance is education and information. That is why when a spirit presents information like this, the medium must present the evidence as objectively as possible.

"Well, I'm blown away!" Jolene said. "We live in Gramma's house, and the wiring is really old. Last week my husband was in the basement looking at the fuse box, and he told me we needed to have the house rewired."

"Pogo stick," I blurted out at the appearance of another image. "Don't get a pogo stick."

Jolene started to laugh. "Oh my gosh! My husband and I were watching TV, and we saw a clip about some kid on a pogo stick. We wondered how we ever did that as kids ourselves."

"I'm getting that Gramma doesn't like pogo sticks," I conveyed.

"She was adamant about me not having a pogo stick as a child. Wow! Between the wiring and the pogo stick, it sure looks like she's still watching over me!"

SHAKESPEARE WROTE, "BE not afraid of greatness; some men are born great, some achieve greatness, and others have greatness thrust upon them." It's no surprise that fame and fortune are the driving influences for many people in the material world. Of course we don't see U-Hauls behind hearses, but does being famous live on in the eternal consciousness after physical death?

Vera was visiting Florida from her home in Australia. Although she was American, she had emigrated to the "Land Down Under." She was an attractive middle-aged woman dressed in an understated yet elegant manner. Vera had a very warm and engaging personality and told me that she'd read several books about spirit contact, including my book *Never Letting Go*.

As the reading began, I told her, "The energy of a man is coming through. He was definitely an alpha male—in control and accustomed to giving orders and being in charge," I described.

"That's Father," Vera replied.

"He's depicting himself wearing a tuxedo—tail coat, white shirt, and bow tie. His hair is slicked back. It looks like he stepped out of a Hollywood movie from the 1930s! Actually, he looks like Clark Gable."

"Oh! Father so loved it when people compared his looks to Clark Gable's. Father was very dashing and debonair," Vera shared.

"Hey! I recognize your father," I said as I mentioned his name. (Vera's father was a famous billionaire; to respect the family's privacy, I agreed not to disclose his name in this book.)

"That is Father! Mark, this is so nice. Do you see him with anyone?"

"Well, yes, hold on..." I said as another spirit adjusted his frequency so I could perceive him. "There's another male with him."

"Do go on," Vera said with a smile.

"It looks like they're both standing on a golf course. Hmmm...this guy looks familiar too! I know I've seen him before—oh, okay…he looks like a young version of Ronald Reagan," I explained.

"Oh, how lovely!" Vera exclaimed. "Father and President Reagan used to play golf together."

"Excuse me?" I interrupted. "Your father knew President Ronald Reagan?"

"Oh, but of course! When we lived in California and Ronny was governor, the two of them played golf all the time. He was a lovely man." Vera sat back in her chair, looking very pleased.

"So…I'm talking to Ronald Reagan?"

"Sounds like it. Do carry on, Mark," Vera requested quite casually.

"Oh, okay. Uh, and now I see two other people coming through, a man and a woman," I described.

"Really? Can you tell who they are?" Vera asked.

"Hold on—they don't feel like family…" I hesitated. "This is going to sound nuts, but I recognize these people too."

"Do tell!" Vera said, her excitement obvious.

I continued, "I saw this documentary on the History Channel and these people look like—and I know this sounds bizarre—but they look like King Edward VIII and Wallis Simpson," I said after a short pause.

"Oh, *them*," Vera remarked with a hint of disgust.

"Your father knew them?" I asked.

"Oh yes, but he couldn't stand them. He felt they were total freeloaders—always showing up at our parties and always expecting someone else to pick up the tab. All because he'd been King of England and gave up the throne for *her*," Vera noted, a bit unhappily.

"Seriously?" I wanted confirmation. "King Edward and Wallis Simpson?"

"That woman was such a shameless social climber! I remember them coming to our house when I was very young. Father always resented them. Couldn't understand the King's attraction to her," Vera revealed.

"Vera, now let me get this straight. I'm talking to your father—a famous billionaire—and President Ronald Reagan, King Edward VIII, and Wallis Simpson?" I couldn't hide my incredulity.

"Of course you are, dear, Father knew them all!" she touted.

"Well!" I said, taking a deep breath and focusing back on the energy of these spirits. "Your father wants you to know that he's resolved his differences with Edward and Wallis, President Reagan says hello, and that he loves you."

"Smashing! I'm delighted to hear this," Vera said cheerfully.

WHILE TOURING PENNSYLVANIA, I was invited to be a guest on a popular morning radio talk show. Malia, the host of the morning show, turned out to be one of the most amazing people I've ever met. She was more than a talk show host: she was politically involved, a voice for the underprivileged, and a leader in the African-American community.

As the interview started that morning, it appeared Malia was skeptical of interdimensional communication. However, the phone lines became jammed as I took calls and conducted mini readings for listeners. Malia watched me intently during the show. I could see some of her skepticism giving way to belief.

After the show, Malia asked if I would conduct a reading for her, and I was happy to oblige. One of the radio station's producers showed Rocky and me to a conference room where I could conduct the reading. The producer wanted to observe the reading as well, and we welcomed her. I started with prayers and then opened up to frequency.

"The first man coming through is an older African-American gentleman. It seems he was quite elderly when he passed. He apparently had lots of physical problems," I told Malia.

"That's not unusual for older people," Malia responded. Ever the interviewer and still skeptical, it was clear she wanted specifics.

"It feels like a burning sensation in his lungs, most likely cancer. Also, there were circulation issues in his extremities. It seems like he was heavily medicated for the pain prior to passing, but his mind was still sharp and he was struggling to maintain lucidity," I described.

"So far, so good. What else do you get about him?" she asked.

"He appears connected to you through your mother's side of the family—like a maternal grandfather." I looked at Malia, who nodded.

"My mother's father died of lung cancer," she confirmed.

"Smart man, a good mind. He seemed very worldly, like he had traveled a lot and...and..." I was stunned at what I perceived.

"And what?" Malia asked calmly. Her striking green eyes gazed into mine.

"He's with someone," I continued.

"You said they're never alone on the Other Side. Why is it so unusual to see him with someone?" Malia, ever the radio journalist, surfaced again.

"Well, the man he is with looks like...Mahatma Gandhi." I expected Malia to react with surprise. The producer and Rocky looked at me as if I'd just sprouted a second head.

Malia, however, maintained her cool and calm demeanor. "My grandfather lived in India in the 1930s. He studied non-violent civil disobedience under Gandhi. My grandfather and Mahatma Gandhi were good friends. I'm happy to hear they still are," she explained.

"Do you mean that I'm—I'm communicating with Gandhi? *The* Gandhi? Mohandas K. Gandhi...the Mahatma? Why, he's one of my heroes! The greatest spiritual leader since St. Francis of Assisi!" I almost jumped out of my seat.

"Why not? They were close friends. It makes sense they'd come in together—and besides, that's something you couldn't possibly have known ahead of time. This proves to me that it really is my grandfather," she responded with a smile.

I sat back in my chair, overwhelmed and humbled by the energies of these two great souls.

Malia continued, "My grandfather left India in the late 1940s after India's independence from Britain. He was instrumental in the civil rights movement here in the United States during the 1960s. He believed the key to change is through peace and nonviolence," Malia explained.

As Rocky and I left the station after the reading, I took Malia's hand. "Thank you for one of the great honors of my life, Malia: to touch not only your grandfather's energy but, for a moment, to be in the presence of Gandhi."

"The pleasure was all mine. Thank you for reuniting my grandfather and me. He meant the world to me," Malia replied with graceful elegance.

Two weeks later, I received a telephone call from the radio station producer who had sat in during the reading. She was very upset. Malia, who was only fifty-four years old, had collapsed and died suddenly of a heart attack. The producer thought I would want to know.

I was devastated. Although I'd only met her once, I felt I'd lost a dear friend. I had seen Malia as one of those remarkable people who made a positive difference in the lives of those she met. Her loss reminded me that each of us is unique and influences the people around us. Our mission in the material world is to learn and share.

Malia's light seemed to glow just a little bit brighter than most. Although I was saddened by her loss, on a spiritual level

I realized she was so much more than the finite confines of her physical body. Who and what she was would live on in eternity. Her soul's energetic consciousness had been released, and highly evolved and loving spirits would greet and guide her into the Light.

10

Homicide and the
Other Side of Justice

As both a prosecuting attorney and a criminal defense lawyer, I have tried criminal cases ranging from misdemeanors to murders. The material world's legal system is far from perfect. I've seen justice done at the conclusion of a jury trial when someone wrongfully accused is found innocent. I've also witnessed the truly guilty go free. However, there are repercussions to committing homicide that go far beyond our material world existence. The Other Side has many different levels for a reason, and as a medium I recognize that there is no escaping the evil one commits in the material world.

What does it take to kill another human being? Is it a complete abandonment of all sense of decency, compassion, human feeling, and love? Is it the act of an unbalanced mind? Is it an act of momentary rage committed in the heat of passion? Is it the calculating plan of a predator? Is it the unintentional act of a negligent person who never intended to inflict death upon another? Is it ever justifiable, such as when a parent defends the life of a child?

Homicide is such a complex behavior that the legal system of every nation in the world is filled with laws about it. These laws encompass a vast array of concepts, from determining the intent of the accused, the mental competence of the accused, the degrees and types of homicide, defenses that may exonerate a killer, and the sentences regulating punishment for the guilty. For the most part, homicide committed intentionally is prosecuted as a criminal offense. In other instances, taking the life of another person may be deemed accidental or justified by legal concepts such as self-defense or necessity, like a soldier's duty during time of war.

There is no one reason people commit homicide. However, my work as an attorney and as a medium has given me insights into why some people do. I have observed how grief leads to crime, which leads to grief. The key to homicide may lie in death itself.

Failure to cope with the death of a loved one in a healthy manner can cause grief to fester within a person. Grief cannot be avoided, suppressed, or numbed away by drugs and alcohol. Grief has an insidious way of resurfacing in the form of behaviors that often result in criminal activity, including rage, physical and sexual aggression, drug and alcohol addiction, predator behavior, and even murder. This is why it's extremely important to cope with grief, especially for a child or young adult. It is difficult enough for adults to cope with the death of a loved one, but for a child or young adult without the life experience and emotional skill set to deal with death, the results can be disastrous.

I came across a case involving an eleven-year-old boy. At first blush, he was a model son and student. He did well in school and seemed happy, outgoing, personable, and artistically inclined. He was a devout Catholic who loved to sing in his church's choir. He admired the ritual and pageantry of the Catholic Church and even dreamed of one day becoming a priest.

Then his little brother died suddenly of complications from measles. This death severely affected the child. He became disruptive in school, argued constantly with his authoritative father, and became emotionally distant from family and friends. His parents did little or nothing to counsel their son or help him cope with his grief. Instead, they told him he'd grow out of it.

Three years later, the boy's father died suddenly. Although his relationship with his father had been strained, this loss sent him further into the throes of grief. Now a teenager, his attitude went from bad to worse. He grew increasingly aggressive and disrespectful toward authority and became an even more severe behavior problem in school. In one impulsive act of rebellion against his teachers, he took his school certificate—considered an important document—and used it as toilet paper. This bizarre act of disrespect prompted the school director to expel him from school.

Angry and directionless, the teenager clung to the only meaningful relationship remaining in his life, that with his mother. Four years later, when he was seventeen years old, she was diagnosed with an aggressive form of cancer. Despite the doctor's poor prognosis, her son insisted she undergo an experimental cancer treatment. Reluctantly, she agreed and died as a result of the treatment. Reeling from her death and consumed by guilt, the young man spiraled downward into his grief, which took the form of anger, hatred, and a particular thirst for violence. His name was Adolf Hitler.

While it is difficult to feel pity for Hitler, one could ask the question: was the criminal born or was the criminal created? His vitriolic hatred had to start somewhere. From a clinical standpoint, Hitler certainly makes the case, albeit an extreme one, that grief leads to crime, which leads to grief. It is a very real possibility that his unresolved issues with grief led to the ultimate criminality that later inflicted unspeakably horrific grief upon millions.

From a humanistic view, we can only wonder what might have been the result had he been given the benefit of grief counseling or raised by loving and supportive parents. While we will never know the answer in the case of Adolf Hitler, I have seen circumstances where despite horrific tragedy in the developmental years of a child, hope, personal fortitude, and determination can prevail.

During my legal career, I've encountered thousands of people with substance abuse problems. I've never met a happy alcoholic or drug addict. Becoming an addict doesn't happen without a reason. Most of those affected don't wake up one day and say, "Gee, everything in my life is so fulfilled and happy. I feel so loved—I think I'll start shooting up heroin!"

My experience has shown that for many, the root cause of unhappiness stems from an unresolved death of a loved one. This does not mean people who are abusers all end up as murderers. However, substance abuse is often an avoidance behavior. People who are unhappy with themselves or their lives avoid coping with their unhappiness through drug and alcohol dependence.

I FIRST MET Dean when he was sixteen years old and charged with possession of alcohol by a minor. His father, Sammy, a retired New York State corrections officer, retained my services as an attorney to defend Dean. Both father and son projected outgoing and gregarious personas, yet beneath their façades I sensed a great darkness within both of them.

As Dean got older, his alcohol problem grew worse. He drank so much he would black out and have absolutely no memory of what had happened while he was drinking. His alcoholism resulted in two arrests for drunk driving. Due to the blackouts, he couldn't recall any of the details associated with the arrest. It was a miracle he never killed himself or anyone else while he was driving in such a highly intoxicated condition.

After his second arrest for drunk driving, Dean finally decided to quit drinking. He met a wonderful woman and they married and had a son. It looked as if his life was finally beginning to take a happy turn for the better.

Unfortunately, not long after his son's second birthday, Dean's father, Sammy, was diagnosed with severe lung cancer. Dean stayed by his father's side during Sammy's long and painful death from cancer.

I was concerned Sammy's death might act as a trigger for Dean to start drinking again. As a lawyer, my job is to defend criminals' constitutional rights or find them help so they don't commit future crimes. As a medium, I try to help people heal from the pain of loss so they don't engage in impulsive behaviors. It was time for me to have a talk with Dean, not as a lawyer but as a medium—and, more importantly, as a friend. I called Dean and asked to meet with him.

Dean entered my office and sat down. He was no longer the wild-eyed teenager I'd met so many years ago. Before me was a man in his thirties who was a husband, father, college graduate, and extremely talented Internet technician.

"I appreciate you asking me here, Mark, and I suspect you're going to tell me to be careful about my drinking. Trust me, I don't want to ever see the inside of a jail cell again," Dean told me.

"Thanks, Dean, you just saved me ten minutes of preaching," I joked.

"Mark, I know you're a medium and can communicate with spirits." Dean clearly had his own agenda. "Maybe one day I'll want to make a connection with my father, but I'm just not ready now."

"No problem; I understand completely. I don't impose interdimensional communication on anyone," I assured him. Because of his technical background, Dean had enjoyed my explanation of frequency, vibration, and the more scientific aspects of spirit communication in our past conversations.

"You've probably been wondering why I drank," Dean volunteered, handing me a letter. "This will explain it. It's to the Parole Board of New York."

"Do you have a case in New York you haven't told me about? As your lawyer, Dean, I need to know everything that's going on with you legally," I chided.

"Don't worry, I'm not in any legal trouble." Dean watched silently as I began to read his letter.

To the New York State Division of Parole:

When I was six years old, two days before my seventh birthday, I was at home in my room. My mother was downstairs, and my brother, Scott, was there with his friend Matt. I knew my brother's friend was not supposed to be there.

A few minutes later, I heard a gunshot. My mother screamed, so I ran out of my room and saw Matt and Scott tossing a handgun back and forth. My mother demanded they give her the gun. I saw Matt point the gun at her and pull the trigger. My brother Scott yelled, "We did it!"

In a flash, the world of a six-year-old was destroyed. In shock, I cried, "You killed my mommy!"

Scott and Matt rolled her up in the rug and left her there on the floor. Scott grabbed me and forced me into his car. I was kidnapped by my own brother. He tried to take me out of state, but his car got stuck in the mud along the interstate. Luckily, a police officer spotted the car. I only remember him as Trooper Dave. I always wondered what Scott had planned for me, but I'm sure it wasn't going to have a happy ending.

My childhood and my life shattered like glass. I've been in therapy since I was seven years old. I have nightmares and more sleepless nights than I can remember. In a lifetime of therapy, medication, and substance abuse, I can verify that you cannot talk it out and they don't make a pill that allows you to function, be happy, and get over something like this. No matter how much I cry it out, the grief seems to "reload."

By age twelve, I was placed in a psychiatric facility for two years. I started drinking hard liquor the day I got out at fourteen. This transformed me into an alcoholic who rationalized that numbing myself with alcohol let me forget for a little while.

I loathe holidays and celebrations because of my pain. I hate my birthday most of all. I can't enjoy life and this has negatively impacted every relationship I've ever had. I generally feel very distant and guarded from everyone, even my wife.

Matt and Scott destroyed my father. Dad was a captain in NYC Corrections. That day he came home from work and found the love of his life rolled up in a carpet and his children missing destroyed him.

We were so traumatized and hurt, we rarely spoke of what happened. He worked his ass off, usually fourteen hours a day, just to avoid his reality. We could not share any kinds of memories because it was too painful. I do not really know my family history. Dad was so depressed, he never went out or even considered another woman for the remainder of his life. He essentially committed suicide by smoking excessively until his death from lung cancer at fifty-six.

Matt's and Scott's sentences are twenty-five years to life. My sentence is much worse because it is a life sentence of depression and agony. I honestly hope that the Parole Board will consider the heinous nature of this crime and its far-reaching consequences.

I have made it my duty to ensure the life portion of this twenty-five-to-life sentence is carried out. Please show me there really is justice in this world and deny parole for these killers.

"Good lord; I don't know what to say," I managed to convey as the full impact of his letter engulfed me.

"What can you say? What can anyone say?" Dean asked me. "I've been living with this my whole life. It has brought me to the brink of suicide—and even worse."

"Yet somehow you've managed to remain sober for some years now," I replied.

"The last time you represented me for drunk driving, I was so wasted. I didn't remember even getting behind the wheel of my car that night. All I remember is waking up in a jail cell the next day—and with a monster hangover."

"What are you saying, Dean?"

"Do you have any idea how many times I've thought about what if I had killed someone? Someone's mother or child or wife? Then *I'd* be the monster! *I'd* be the one who destroyed someone's life like my own brother and his friend did to my father and me! And that is something I cannot allow to happen!"

"Your grief led to alcoholism, and that led you to committing the crime of drunk driving, and that very easily could have led to killing a person and inflicting the horror of grief on someone else," I repeated.

"Mark, I know there is hell! It is here on earth, and I've been in it since the day my mother was murdered. One thing is certain: I can't let them win. If I cave in and continue drinking…if I abuse my son or my wife…if I commit suicide, then they've won—and that must never happen."

"It seems you're working hard to emerge from hell," I observed with a look of admiration.

"If I don't work toward resolving my anger—if I don't find a way to heal from this prison of pain and grief—then I will always be its prisoner, and I've been in this hellish prison long enough!" Dean said emphatically. "Someday, I want to go to see my brother in prison. I want to ask him, why didn't you walk away? What were you thinking? What did our mother do to you? What did I do to you to deserve having every day of the rest of my life affected?"

"You know, Dean, connecting with the spirits of your parents might help you move on with this," I offered.

"I know it will, but they're in heaven—and he's here. They don't need to explain why this happened; he does. I want him to look me straight in the eye while he's in our world and not on the Other Side. It will take everything I've got to confront him, but until then, I've still got a lot of work to do. I want—no, I *deserve* to have a happy life! I want to know what it is to actually feel joy, not just stress, aggravation, and misery!"

I listened carefully, knowing how important it was for Dean to articulate these feelings.

"Every day of my life is a battle, and I pray it is a battle I can win."

"It sounds to me like you are well on your way to winning this war," I remarked.

"I'm trying to learn to cope with grief so I can go from being its victim to being its volunteer. Sound familiar?" Dean remarked with a wry smile.

"Yes, I've heard that one before," I replied, humbled that he'd read that in my book.

The last I heard from Dean, he was still sober and doing well as a computer specialist. He has not yet visited his brother, who remains in prison.

Addiction is an affliction that is difficult to conquer. Personal growth is often a choice requiring pain and sacrifice. Dean's decision to stop drinking and concentrate on being a good father and husband would require both. He knew that returning to the emptiness of alcoholism and collapsing into the pain of grief would be a far more difficult and dangerous path.

J. R. R. TOLKIEN WROTE, "All we have to decide is what to do with the time that is given us." We have free will, which is the ability to decide. Intentionally committed homicide is an exercise of free will. Sometimes, though, a person doesn't make a conscious decision to kill another but makes reckless decisions that tragically result in a death.

Gordon was curious, albeit somewhat skeptical, about interdimensional communication. When his maternal grandfather made contact, it was clear this was the connection he wanted.

"Your grandfather was an elderly man. For some reason, he's adamant about his feet! They are somehow tied to his death, which feels sudden and unexpected," I described. "Strange, I am having this odd sensation—like something is splitting in two. His death occurred at night, didn't it?"

"That makes a lot of sense," Gordon confirmed. "My grandfather was killed at night. He was crossing the street when a car hit him right in front of the retirement community where he lived. The speed limit there is 25 miles per hour and a car speeding at 70 miles per hour hit him. I know why you are feeling that his feet are so significant. That splitting in two you mentioned has to do with the fact that he was hit so hard by the car, it cut his legs off at the knees. His torso flew up over the hood and through the windshield of the car. The top part of his body landed in the back seat."

Distressed by Gordon's graphic description, I said, "I'm so sorry."

"Do you get anything about the woman who killed my grandpa?"

"Yes, I'm receiving an image of a young woman. She was barely in her twenties, and she had an olive-skinned complexion, dark eyes, and long, wiry hair."

"She was from Ecuador," Gordon responded. "And can you tell how she died?"

It surprised me that Gordon would ask, but immediately I felt a sharp jolt. "Ouch! I'm experiencing a sharp pain in my head."

"She died of a brain tumor," Gordon shared.

"She's so sorry," I conveyed. "She is saying, 'In life I tried to avoid responsibility for this accident. I tried to say it wasn't my fault. I tried to blame it on your grandfather for not looking where he was going.'"

"That's true," Gordon explained. "She was charged with vehicular homicide, and she kept rejecting the plea offers made by the prosecutors. She always said it was Grandpa's fault. She switched lawyers three times—kept saying she wanted a trial. Finally, at the last moment, the prosecutor chickened out and offered a plea to a reduced charge. She only got eight months for killing my grandfather!"

"Although she played the victim, she never forgave herself and created her own hell here on earth. She didn't intentionally kill your grandfather, but the guilt gnawed at her unrelentingly." I could feel this woman's remorse.

Gordon listened thoughtfully. "Interesting. Eventually, she did apologize—at the end of her life."

"'For every action there is an equal and opposite reaction,'" I commented, quoting Sir Isaac Newton.

"You mean like with the laws of physics?" Gordon asked.

"Exactly like that. God created a law of balance. Some people refer to this as karma. Essentially, everything you do comes back to you. If you do something good, it comes back to you. If you commit a negative act, it comes back on you. Whether here in the material world or on the Other Side, no one can avoid the law of karma," I explained.

"Apparently not," Gordon agreed. "It's as if her guilt was transformed into the cancer that slowly ate her to death an inch at a time. She sent word to my family through hospice that she was sorry. She believed her guilt and the blame she placed on herself gave her cancer."

"Gordon, wait! Your grandfather is projecting another message! He's standing at the top of a green hill on a beautiful sunny day. The young woman is below him at the bottom of the hill," I described.

"What's that mean?"

"Your grandfather is demonstrating that he's in a higher frequency on the Other Side—it's the heaven dimension, and the woman is, well, not in the same dimension. She resides in a lower frequency. You see, there are levels to the Other Side. Those who bring pain and harm cross over to the Other Side, but they go to a lower frequency, on a level that is farther from the Light." I hoped Gordon could understand the concept of levels on the Other Side.

"Do you mean she's in hell?" Gordon asked.

"It's more of a purgatory as opposed to the eternal damnation of hellfire and brimstone we were frightened into believing as children. Due to our finite physical form, it's hard for us to fully comprehend the infinity of the Other Side. The Light is the spiritual energy of God, and those who are on the Other Side in an absence of the Light—well, they don't experience the joy and peace one has in the presence of God. Those spirits must work to atone for the evil they've done in order to rise to the higher frequency on the Other Side."

"Wow, that's interesting!" Gordon seemed fascinated.

"Your grandfather is reaching out to this woman and pulling her up to the top of the hill with him. He's welcoming her to the higher frequency, and now she's standing next to him."

Gordon sat quietly.

"Your grandfather has tremendous compassion and sympathy for the woman who killed him. He's putting his arm around her shoulder and he's saying, 'I know she didn't mean it, and when you are ready, forgive her—I do.'"

"Grandpa was so loving and gentle." Gordon looked down. "Seems like free will is something we have in our world and in the world to come. He's chosen to forgive her; I guess that's why he's in heaven. I know I have to make the choice to forgive. I may be getting to the point where I can.

"Grandpa was very wise," Gordon reflected. "He once told me that we must never take consolation in the suffering of others. The woman who killed him suffered a slow and painful death from cancer. While it doesn't make me feel any better, somehow it seems justice was done."

AS A PROFESSIONAL medium, I've developed the ability to control when I'm open to the frequency of spirits and when I'm not. If a medium doesn't control this, it can be distracting because spirits will constantly try making contact. Despite my discipline, spirits who want to make contact will—and sometimes when I least expect it.

During a book promotion tour in New York City, I was scheduled for an interview with Dianna Navarro, the host of a popular radio show broadcast from Umberto's Clam House. Rocky and I were excited to visit Umberto's, a famous landmark in Little Italy. Unfortunately for us, it was a freezing cold and rainy February day in Manhattan. Getting a taxi was virtually impossible, so we walked the sixteen blocks to Umberto's in the icy rain.

Shivering and drenched, we stepped happily into the warmth at Umberto's. The aroma of Italian sausages frying in olive oil with peppers, onions, and garlic permeated the air. The cozy restaurant had an old-fashioned bar with a brass railing, a dozen tables with red-and-white checked tablecloths, and a black-and-white tile floor. The gregarious all-male staff ranged in age from twenty to seventysomething.

"This place is like something out of *The Godfather*," Rocky whispered to me after she ordered an espresso and a cup of Italian wedding soup.

"Yeah, you can say that again," I replied, feeling a constriction around my throat.

"Mark! What's wrong?" Rocky asked.

"I'm feeling like someone got strangled here—with a wire around his throat," I said as I excused myself to go the men's room.

"Oh boy!" Rocky murmured, turning to greet Dianna, who had just arrived.

My visit to the men's room didn't make me feel any better. I felt a pain in the back of my head, as if it were being blown off by a gunshot. On my way out of the men's room, I passed the bar and felt a sharp stabbing sensation between my ribs. As I approached our table to greet Dianna, I was stunned by a bashing sensation to my face.

"Mark, are you okay? You're pale as a ghost," Dianna commented as I took my seat.

"Funny you should say that," I replied.

Dianna turned to greet the restaurant staff. "This is Mark Anthony, the psychic lawyer," Dianna said by way of introduction.

"Psychic lawyer? You kiddin' me?" exclaimed one.

"I coulda used you a few years ago!" joked a different guy.

"Yo! Good to meet you," another said.

"Wanna glass of wine?" asked someone else.

"You hungry? Have some clams!" Obviously, hospitality reigned at Umberto's.

I began, "Hey—uh…by any chance, did someone get killed here—in this restaurant?"

All eyes fixed on me. "Why you wanna know?" the manager asked.

"Like Dianna said, I'm a psychic medium, and I pick up on things. I'm sensing that a person, or maybe more than one person, died here," I explained.

"Yeah, lots of guys got whacked here back in the old days," the manager said. The staff responded with raucous laughter.

"That was a long time ago! Nothin' like that happens here anymore," the server said as he brought our drinks. Then he put both his hands on the table and leaned toward me. "Anything else you wanna know?"

"No, everything's fine," I replied, knowing that it hadn't all been fine in the past.

"Relax, Mark—they're having fun with you," Dianna said with a smile and a wink. "They're really good guys."

"More like *GoodFellas!*" Rocky added.

PSYCHIC MEDIUMS ARE often consulted to assist police in murder investigations. Information received through psychic intuition is technically hearsay evidence because it cannot be cross-examined, and there are no exceptions to that rule. Therefore, it is not admissible in a court of law.

Where psychic intuition may be used is behind the scenes. It can help the police understand what did occur at a crime scene, giving them leads for finding evidence, which may help them develop the probable cause necessary for a lawful arrest. While not all police investigators are open to using psychics, it is a far more common practice than is generally known. It's rewarding to see evidence located by intuition used in the prosecution and, sometimes, the conviction of a murderer.

Criminal trials can be dramatic and exciting. However, what many people don't appreciate is that when all the excitement ends, the suffering of the victim's family does not. The trauma a victim's family goes through and the pain inflicted upon them is horrendous. They are unendingly plagued by the grief of their loved one's death and by the gnawing fact that someone intentionally inflicted such agony upon them. It is even more difficult to come to terms with death when it is the result of senseless brutality.

This is why interdimensional communication can be such an important therapeutic step in the healing process. It helps the survivors understand what happened to their loved one, and it also helps them on their journey toward resolution and inner peace. While forgiveness may be the key to inner peace, it is the most complex of all virtues—and the most difficult to attain. Forgiveness can take a lifetime to achieve. And even then, heavenly assistance may be required.

Carlos and Janna were a dignified, reserved couple who came to see me for a reading. They respected my policy of not telling me anything about them or with whom they wanted to communicate. This is a quality control procedure that I believe maintains the integrity of the reading. I don't want to know anything ahead of time that may color the perceptions I receive during the interdimensional communication.

Evidential mediumship requires the client to confirm to the medium if a piece of evidence received from a spirit has been accurately interpreted. Sometimes the significance of the evidence is immediately apparent. Other times, it requires thought and reflection after the reading.

Sitting facing Carlos and Janna, I began, "A young man, like maybe a son, is coming through."

"Yes." Janna nodded solemnly.

"I'm getting that his death was quick and unexpected. It feels violent and very traumatic," I described.

"Yes, we lost our son, Miguel," Carlos confirmed.

"Was there a car involved? Seems like a car was somehow involved," I conveyed.

"No, it wasn't a car accident." Janna shook her head. Even though Janna gave a negative response to the question of a car being involved, somehow I still felt it was. Instead of belaboring the point, I focused on the next wave of frequency emitted from their son's spirit.

"Rapid and labored breathing…he had difficulty breathing." I began to feel respiratory distress.

"That might make sense—I'm not sure." Janna's response was tentative.

"I'm seeing a flash of light! The last thing he saw was a flash of light," I relayed.

They both looked unsure, nodding their heads in confusion.

I continued, "Miguel was a hyperactive person. He had a lot of nervous energy, didn't he? He describes himself as a stick of dynamite on a short fuse!"

"That's an accurate description of him," Carlos agreed, smiling briefly.

"His passing…uh, he said he was at the end of his rope—and his passing feels senseless." I saw Janna shudder at the implication.

"They tied him up!" she exclaimed.

"Now he's showing me the number 7. Does the number 7 make sense?"

"This happened in 2007," Janna said, her face grim.

"And he was kidnapped from a convenience store—a 7-Eleven," Carlos reported. Apparently, the "7" image was a multiple-meaning message.

"I don't know if you're prepared to hear this," I paused. "But I want you to know what I'm hearing. Your son is presenting me with a quote from the Bible: 'Forgive them, for they know not what they do.'"

Carlos looked angry. Janna wiped her eyes and said, "I read that quote in the Bible all the time. No one knows I do that, and I'm trying—I'm really trying to feel forgiveness."

"Your son says, even from a young age, he felt the burdens of the world upon him. Now he has let go. He wants you to know that he is free of the burdens that always felt like weights holding him down. Now he is at peace in the heaven dimension," I shared.

"Our son was bipolar," Janna confided softly. "He always said it was a burden, like a weight holding him down when he wished he could fly—to be free of the mood swings."

"The flash. Earlier you said he saw a flash," Carlos interjected. "They shot him in the face."

"Ah, the last thing he saw was the flash of gunfire going off in his face." It was all beginning to gel.

"His breathing—you said before that he had a problem with his breathing. That does make sense because they tried to suffocate him before he died," Janna said.

As the interdimensional communication progressed, the pieces of evidence presented by their son at the beginning of the session began to fit together. Even though their son let them know he'd attained the inner peace that had so eluded him during his life, Janna and Carlos had carried the shock and trauma caused by the cold-blooded killing for so many years. Miguel's consciousness was fully aware of this and was sympathetic to their feelings.

"Your son is drawing my attention to St. Patrick's Day," I conveyed.

"Our anniversary is on St. Patrick's Day!" Janna exclaimed. Carlos reached for Janna's hand, and her smile lit up the room.

"Happy anniversary from the Other Side," I told them, unable to keep from smiling myself. Some of the pain in their eyes diminished as they felt Miguel's love reaching out to them through heaven's veil.

After the reading, I was presented with a newspaper article about Miguel's murder. The article chronicled how one evening Miguel had driven to a 7-Eleven convenience store. He drove an expensive vehicle, which unfortunately drew the attention of two men with criminal histories. They sparked up an ingratiating conversation with Miguel and eventually managed to lure him to one of their homes. While he was there, Miguel must have sensed their sinister intent. A fight broke out, and Miguel was beaten, subdued, and tied up with a rope.

Miguel's bipolar disorder exacerbated the situation, and one of the criminals became excessively irritated. Instead of acting humanely and setting him free, the criminal tried to smother him with a blanket. When that didn't work, one of them shot Miguel in the face. They wrapped his body in a rug, threw him into the trunk of his own vehicle, drove it into the woods, and set it on fire.

After I read this, it dawned on me that a motor vehicle had indeed been involved—Miguel's.

WHAT IS THE objective of punishment in the legal system? The lawyer in me believes in restraining criminals, the psychic medium in me believes in rehabilitating them, and the human in me believes in exacting revenge.

The United States criminal justice system is far from perfect, yet it is premised upon the accused being innocent until proven guilty in a court of law. An attorney's job is not to judge someone because that person has committed a crime. Laypeople often confuse an attorney's obligation to defend someone as tacit approval of the crime, but nothing could be further from the truth. It is the attorney's obligation to defend the rights of the accused, not to condone or approve of what the accused has done.

After an appearance on *Coast to Coast AM*, a late-night radio talk show broadcast worldwide, I received a letter from a man in prison named Ellis. He faced the death penalty, so I assumed he was charged with a particularly heinous murder.

My suspicions were confirmed when I read in his letter that the charge had been for the first-degree premeditated murder of his father. The record said that Ellis, who was in his early forties, went to his father's home one afternoon demanding money. When his father refused, Ellis took a machete and butchered his father.

I've represented thousands of criminals, and it looked to me like another sad and familiar tale. Drugs like heroin, cocaine, and crystal meth are so powerfully addictive that being deprived of them will cause someone's cravings for these dangerous drugs to escalate to the level of murder. A junkie needs a fix at any cost, even if that means killing someone you love so you can get high for a few hours.

It's easy to despise such a person, even if you've never met him. Somehow it feels right looking down on these kinds of criminals as being a vile, lower form of life. Even though attorneys are supposed to be objective and not rush to judgment, I found myself disgusted by this man and annoyed that he wrote asking for spiritual guidance.

Although I tried to dismiss Ellis from my thoughts, I couldn't. I kept thinking of what one of my mentors, a great trial lawyer, told a jury about a man who was accused of sedition.

"He was brought before the highest legal authority in the land," the attorney said. "His accusers were prominent members of the community, many of them religious leaders—and they demanded vengeance. Even though no credible evidence was presented, the magistrate bowed to mob rule and merely washed his hands of the accused and condemned him to death."

My mentor was talking about Jesus. Even though comparing Jesus to a murderous drug addict seems hard to imagine, I realized that the words "innocent until proven guilty" are more than just a slogan. In our democracy, we have the rule of law; despite what we may think or how guilty someone may seem, we have a Constitution and a legal system, not mob rule that condemns without evidence.

It also dawned on me that a lot of good people have spent time in prison cells. Joan of Arc was found guilty of witchcraft and burned at the stake. This hit home with me in a very personal way since, from all indications, she was a medium who communicated with spirits. Gandhi spent years in prison because he stood up against oppression. Martin Luther King Jr. was arrested and spent time in jail during the civil rights struggle.

And even though he had been sentenced to death, Jesus forgave a fellow prisoner who was crucified beside him, reassuring him that they would see each other in paradise after death.

I called Ellis's attorney at a public defender's office located in a rural county in the state where he was charged. Because I'm an attorney, the receptionist put me right through.

"Hi, I'm Mark Anthony the Psychic Lawyer, and I'm calling about your client Ellis," I said over the phone.

"Psychic what? Is this some kinda joke?" responded the young male attorney in a heavy Southern drawl. He seemed slightly irritated I was taking up his time.

"Psychic Lawyer, and no, this isn't a joke," I replied.

"Yeah? What about Ellis?"

"Ellis wrote me and wanted me to contact you to see if you had any problem if I write to him. He has some questions," I explained.

"Listen up," the lawyer interjected. "Before you go and get yourself into this case, you need to know something. This here's one grisly murder. That boy done chopped his daddy up into a lot of itty-bitty pieces. Why you interested?"

"Well, I'm not really interested in the case—I just wanted to get your permission to write to him and possibly interview him," I explained.

"Boy, lemme make this crystal clear. I won't agree to allow my client to make any statements that can jeopardize his case. I don't want you discussing the facts with him, and I'd sure as hell prefer if you didn't talk to him at all!" With that, he hung up on me.

A week later I received this letter from Ellis:

Dear Mark:

My lawyer said you contacted him but he would not tell me why. I appreciate my lawyer's concern to keep everything confidential, but this is my life and not my lawyer's. I'm seeking peace from within spiritually. I don't expect my lawyer to understand that.

I am not trying to get you involved with my case, as these questions are to help me sleep at night.

1. Has my dad spoken to you?

2. How does forgiveness work with spirits?

My beliefs have changed, but my roots are still from the Bible. Yet I can't believe in hell.

My own pain as I live on this world is more hell than anyone should have to suffer. Yet I have survived more than most people could dream of. God has me here for a purpose.

But I cannot move on until I can understand more about
forgiveness and the afterlife. My dad haunts my dreams, and
I'm powerless to do anything but weep.
    Ellis

My years as a criminal defense attorney have brought me into contact with all sorts of manipulative personalities, from the devious to the psychopathic. It didn't appear that this man was trying to manipulate me. Since I don't practice law in the state where the crime occurred, there was nothing I could do from a legal standpoint anyway. Even though prisons are saturated with illegal drugs, maybe he'd become sober and now, with a clear mind, was reflecting on what he'd done and felt sickened by it.

I prayed to find the right words to write him, and this is what came to me:

Dear Ellis:
    You asked two questions that I will do my best to
answer. The first was whether your father has spoken to me.
Mediumistic ability doesn't work that way. I don't conjure or
summon a spirit. It is the client who brings the spirit to the
reading, not me who summons the spirit.
    Your second question was about how forgiveness works
with the Other Side. Spirits are very forgiving. It is receiving
forgiveness from people here in the material world that is the
challenge, and the greatest challenge of all is forgiving yourself.

I'd like to share with you a lesson in self-forgiveness. One of the most enlightened men who ever lived was Mohandas K. Gandhi. He was known as "the Great Soul," which in Hindi is Mahatma. *After the British pulled out of India, tremendous violence broke out between the Hindus and the Muslims and escalated into all-out war.*

The riots in Calcutta were particularly vicious. Despite his pleas for peace, both the Hindus and the Muslims ignored him, so Gandhi went on a hunger strike. He vowed to die rather than to see the violence continue.

This got the attention of the warring parties. Because he was so beloved as a great spiritual leader of peace and nonviolence, the warring factions called a truce. Despite that, Gandhi wanted proof the truce was not temporary.

A delegation of both Hindus and Muslims visited Gandhi to show they had finally stopped fighting. Although the two factions hated each other, they both revered the Mahatma. They were stunned when they walked into the room where Gandhi lay upon a grass mat. Gandhi was an old man, so frail and weak from hunger he could barely move.

One of the Hindu men stepped forward. His eyes burned with fire. Gandhi's family and friends were alarmed and thought he meant violence, but instead he threw a piece of bread at Gandhi and cried out, "Eat! I will not be responsible for your death. It is too late for me—I am going to hell!"

Calmly Gandhi looked up from the piece of bread and into the Hindu man's eyes and asked, "Why do you think you are going to hell? Only God can make that decision."

"During the riots, my five-year-old son was killed—murdered by Muslims!" The man wept. "So I caught a five-year-old Muslim boy—and I smashed his head into a wall. I killed a little boy! I cannot live with myself. I'm going to hell!"

Silence flooded the crowded room.

"I know a way out of hell," Gandhi said softly.

The Hindu stared at the Mahatma.

"Find a young boy, a Muslim boy—about five years old—whose parents have been killed by Hindus during the riots, and raise him as your own," Gandhi told him.

Tears flowed from the Hindu man's eyes.

"But raise him as a Muslim," Gandhi said.

I do not pretend to understand the vast intricacies of the eternal mind of God. I do not know if anyone does. Perhaps the great souls like Mahatma Gandhi did, but I do not. However, I do know that forgiveness can be achieved. It is something that must come not only from words but from actions flowing from a deep commitment within your heart. And even then, only you and God can know the truth.

Peace be unto you and may God bless you,
Mark Anthony

Ellis wrote me one last time:

All the pain and harm I've caused has made for some very dark days, yet I know God has kept me alive for a purpose.

Thank you for the story about Gandhi. It taught me there is hope and maybe even I can help someone. There are a lot of bruised souls in prison, and I will be in the midst of them. In the same way, I'm sure someone will help me learn how to be a better person, even how to be a friend.

My legal experience has taught me that a murderer facing the death penalty will say or do anything to save his life. Jailhouse Christianity, where one has "seen the light" and become a changed man, is a common and often insincere phenomenon. It is possible Ellis was playing games with me and telling me what he thought I wanted to hear.

Then again, judging what actually lies in someone's heart is not my province. Did sobriety lead him to the realization that there is no escaping the evil one commits in the material world? Was he terrified by the prospect of what awaits him on the Other Side? Or was he, like the Hindu man who confessed to murdering an innocent child, seeking a way out of hell?

11

Suicide and
the Other Side

S uicide is much more than just self-inflicted homicide; it's
an extremely complex and painful act with far-reaching
repercussions. Suicide isn't about shame or tarnishing one's
reputation; it is a horrific tragedy. Anyone touched by suicide
understands that it is a life sentence of enduring pain for the
survivors.

Suicide leaves the survivors guilt-ridden and besieged by questions about why it happened and how they could have prevented it from happening. It leaves open questions as to what happens to a spirit on the Other Side who cuts short his or her material world life.

The news media is saturated with stories about murder. News coverage of murder trials has evolved into a twisted form of entertainment. From the nineteenth-century murder trial of accused ax murderer Lizzie Borden to the trial of Bruno Hauptman, accused of kidnapping and murdering the Lindbergh baby, to the O. J. Simpson murder trial and beyond, these cases have captivated modern imagination.

Suicides, though, are much more prevalent in our society. According to the World Health Organization, nearly one million people die by suicide every year. Data compiled by the *American Journal of Public Health* concluded that in the United States alone, more people die from suicide than from car crashes, yet suicide seldom fills the news the way murder does. Why? Is it taboo? Is it a source of embarrassment? Is it the proverbial pink elephant in the room that everyone chooses to ignore?

DESPITE THE SOCIETAL stigma associated with suicide, no one is immune from it. Suicide is a behavior pattern that affects all levels of society, without regard for race, creed, ethnicity, or socioeconomic status. It affects all of us, including me.

Billy and I met in school when we were both eleven years old. Our birthdays were a week apart. Best friends, we were together from junior high through high school and then on to college. When I went to law school, Billy moved to Australia. From there, he proceeded to travel throughout the Far East and learned to speak Indonesian, Thai, and Japanese. For some years he lived in Tokyo and taught English to corporate executives.

One of the great adventures of my life was visiting Billy in Asia. Together we traveled through Japan and hiked the jungles of Thailand. Billy thought it fascinating that I gravitated to the Buddhist temples and engaged the monks in discussions about God and the afterlife. He was curious about my belief that God is everywhere and in all of us, and that we are all a part of God.

This was a continuation of a lifelong debate about God, life after death, and spirit communication, which had begun between us in high school. Billy, also raised Catholic, rejected his faith and became an atheist. I, of course, always advocated the existence of both God and the afterlife. Ever the existentialist, Billy doubted the existence of God but told me that I always gave him something to think about.

Years later Billy moved back to the United States with the love of his life, Yuki, a beautiful woman from Japan. When he met her, she drove a Suzuki. She loved Billy and his off-the-wall sense of humor, even when he called her Yuki Suzuki. Billy had never been so happy in his life.

As a notary public I have the legal authority to marry people, and I was honored when Billy and Yuki asked me to preside at their wedding ceremony. They wrote their own vows. Yuki quoted Lao Tzu. Billy, always the comedian, quoted Groucho Marx.

If you're lucky, you get one friend like Billy in your lifetime. He and I always kept in touch, whether we lived across town or across the world from each other. After their wedding, Billy and Yuki moved to California.

It seemed that Billy had finally found the happiness he'd always sought. He had a loving wife, two young boys, a thriving business as an investment broker, and a beautiful house in Southern California. Sadly, happiness slipped away from him as his parents became extremely ill. His mother fell prey to Alzheimer's disease, and his father was diagnosed with terminal lung cancer. Then the economy collapsed, and the stock market plummeted.

The messages I received from Billy indicated he was not coping well with the downturn in his life. The pressure of dying parents, a young family, and losing a lot of money in the market were overwhelming. And then one day I received a call from Yuki that Billy was in intensive care, clinging to life from a suicide attempt as a result of a drug overdose.

"The doctors told me there is no hope for Billy," Yuki told me tearfully. "They want me to agree to remove life support."

"What did you tell them?"

"I cannot! I know what they are telling me, but I cannot kill Billy."

It took all of my strength to maintain a clear mind and calm demeanor.

"I have no one else to turn to—please help me, Mark," Yuki pleaded in a whisper.

My heart was breaking. I prayed to God with all my might for guidance. My prayer received an answer, which I communicated to Yuki.

"Don't do it. It's your decision, Yuki. Don't give in to pressure. If you aren't ready to make the decision to remove life support, then don't do it," I advised through tears.

Three hours later, Billy expired. He accomplished what he had attempted and died of his own accord. When I received word of his death, I told my secretary to cancel all my appointments, and I went home. My best friend was gone.

Questions flooded my consciousness. What led Billy to the conclusion that suicide was the only way out of his reality? Was it a rational decision? Was his intellect compromised by drugs and alcohol? Was it an impulsive act? Was it a combination of things?

Then, suddenly, I felt a tingling sensation accompanied by a state of heightened awareness. A spirit was making contact. I looked up from my tears and saw the spirit of my mother, Jeannie. Apparently she'd felt the frequency beacon of grief I was emitting and was reaching across heaven's veil to comfort me. I realized she wasn't alone when I saw Billy's spirit standing next to her.

"I guess you won that argument," he told me. Then he smiled, and they both receded from my perception.

It dawned on me that Billy and Yuki had come all the way from California for my mother's funeral. She always regarded him as another son. Then I couldn't help but chuckle, thinking that was so like Billy to make jokes even at the most inappropriate times. It was also a multiple-meaning message. He was reaching out to comfort me and let me know that God and the afterlife exist, and that I was right about the reality of spirit communication. On the other hand, I couldn't help being skeptical, wondering if this had been a figment of my imagination.

An hour later the phone rang. It was my friend, mentor, and fellow medium Lydia. She called to ask if I would like to attend a seminar she was presenting. Just hearing her voice was a welcome relief from my sadness. Before I could say anything about Billy, Lydia asked, "Did a man with blond hair and blue eyes, someone like a brother to you, pass recently?"

"Yes!" I exclaimed, excited this was happening.

"He says he wasn't in his right mind when he did it, and he's sorry. He's very concerned about his wife, and especially how his oldest son will take this," she relayed.

"He has two boys. One is four years old; the other is an infant. Anything else, Lydia?"

"I'm getting something about you winning an argument—it must be some kind of inside joke!" Lydia's voice told me she was smiling into the telephone. True to form, even though he admitted I'd won the argument about the afterlife, Billy still had to have the last word.

EVERYONE IS UNIQUE, and that is why no one theory can explain the reasons someone chooses to voluntarily terminate his or her life. There are, however, trends and patterns that can help us understand what to look for before someone we love commits suicide. Assistance is also available from across heaven's veil. In my work as a medium, I've observed how a spirit can give us insight into why a suicide was committed.

While living in the material world, we are limited to our finite perceptions. A person may perceive he or she has become a prisoner of circumstances so unbearably painful, it is literally hell on earth. Suicide is seen by the victim as the only solution to a reality from which there is no other escape.

For example, in the first chapter, Reed described the horror of witnessing people jumping to their deaths from the World Trade Center on September 11. These people didn't want to die but realized that the circumstances meant they were going to die. While jumping to their deaths would be terrifying, it was preferable to being burned alive. For them, tragically, suicide was the only solution from which there was no other escape.

On an individual level, someone might feel every bit as trapped as the victims who died on September 11. While this person may not be facing a fiery inferno, the perceived reality of that person is so painful that he or she actually feels totally helpless in what is believed by that person to be a hopeless situation.

MELINDA WAS A high school art teacher who met with me for a reading. The spirit of a young man immediately made contact.

"I feel a choking sensation—somehow it feels self-inflicted," I described to Melinda.

"That doesn't make sense with anyone in my family," Melinda responded.

"This person had a physically small stature…very sensitive—seems like he might have been gay," I described.

"Oh my god!" Melinda exclaimed. "That was a student of mine from ten years ago! You're right, he was a very sensitive boy."

"He says they wouldn't stop…they would never let him alone," I conveyed.

Melinda's eyes filled with tears. "Boys made fun of him and called him names. He used to confide in me."

"He felt there was no way out."

Melinda sighed. "I told the school principal about the bullying, but she wouldn't listen. She said kids needed to learn how to stand up for themselves. And sadly, the boy's parents wouldn't listen either. They were in total denial about their son."

I continued, "The spider—the black and red spider. He keeps repeating this image to me."

"Yes, during one assignment in art class, he drew a picture of a spider in a web. It was red and black," Melinda recalled. "It was dark and disturbing. At that moment, I sensed a change in him. He seemed so withdrawn."

"And 'she was the last straw'—does that make sense?" I asked Melinda.

"Yes, it does. This girl, a cheerleader, called him and said, 'Let's get together.' But when he accepted, she laughed at him and said, 'Are you crazy? Me? Go out with a queer?'"

"That's really cruel."

"He came to my classroom after school and told me about it. I could see he'd been crying. He said he just couldn't take it anymore," Melinda said. "This boy lived in a large two-story house known for its elaborate staircase. Later that day, his parents came home and found him hanging from the second-story balustrade overlooking the living room—and the picture he'd drawn of the spider web lay on the floor at the foot of the stairs."

"Well, he wants to thank you for being the only one who listened—and for making a difference now," I conveyed.

"He knows?" Melinda asked.

"He says you make a difference."

Melinda went on, "I couldn't let his death be in vain. I started an anti-bullying group at the school. We met a lot of resistance at first, but we stuck with it—and it expanded to other schools."

Those who choose to commit suicide believe they're victims of a painful reality from which there is no escape out of the earthly hell other than suicide. Tragically, a bullied child often feels this way. Observe and be aware of what is happening with your child. Is your child the victim of a bully? Is your child a bully? Awareness of bullying is the first step to its solution. While a single group at one school may seem small at first, the avalanche of change begins with the fall of a single pebble.

WHILE THERE MAY never be a way to eliminate suicide, there are signs that might indicate when someone close to you is suicidal. In most cases, suicide is a planned event. The person contemplating suicide has given it a lot of thought. One of the clearest signs is talking about it. If someone talks about committing suicide, that person is thinking about it. While there are verbal clues that indicate suicidal ideation, expressions of one's feelings and intentions come in many forms. Someone may express suicidal intent through nonverbal means as well.

Lisa was seen acting suspiciously near the top of a high bridge during rush hour traffic. Several drivers called the police on their cell phones to report her unusual behavior. When confronted by the police, she forcibly resisted and was taken into custody.

The Baker Act is a law in Florida that allows for an involuntary mental examination of a person who is deemed to be in personal danger or dangerous to another person. After an evaluation at a county mental health facility, a psychiatrist determined that Lisa was a suicide risk. I represented her in a Baker Act proceeding conducted at the mental health facility.

"Would your client like to testify, Mr. Anthony?" the judge asked.

"I demand to be heard!" Lisa blurted.

"Proceed," the judge said.

"Lisa, you were seen pacing back and forth on the bridge. Why were you doing this?" I asked her.

"I was so frustrated—I couldn't jump," she answered.

I continued, "The police said they found you at the top of the bridge. You could have jumped from there, couldn't you?"

"Well, I thought that's where I wanted to jump from, but it wasn't!" Lisa announced loudly.

"Why did it matter where on the bridge you wanted to jump?" I asked.

"It was all wrong!" Lisa exclaimed. "I picked my spot, but when I got there that day, it was all ruined! They did some work on the bridge, and I needed to get to where the work wasn't finished."

"What work on the bridge are you referring to?"

"The damn state put up a fence on the side of the bridge I was on—and I would've had to climb over it and then jump," Lisa explained.

"You mean there was a suicide barrier on the side of the bridge you were standing on?"

"Yes—a suicide barrier!" Lisa's voice rose. "But on the other side of the bridge there isn't a damn barrier, just the railing—and that's where I wanted to jump! But there were too many cars!"

"What do you mean, 'too many cars'?" the judge interjected.

"I had to cross two lanes of traffic to get to where I wanted to jump—I didn't want to get hit by a car! That's crazy!"

While Lisa's thought processes may seem irrational, this exchange provides insight into the mind of someone who is suicidal. Lisa was depressed and angry because she felt she had no control over her life. She could, however, control how she would commit suicide. In her mind, she had planned a quick and painless death. Being hit by a car, on the other hand, would be painful, bloody, and messy.

Another way of viewing Lisa's actions is to consider her expression of suicidal intent. She chose a very public place as a result of her desire for someone to notice her and listen to her plight. She received that attention from anonymous drivers who called the police to report her agitated and nervous behavior. While this may not be the sympathetic ear to the proverbial stranger on a bus, it served the same purpose: it gave her validation that someone, somewhere, cared.

If you find yourself in a situation where you observe a stranger acting in a suspicious or irrational manner, please do not try to handle it yourself. If a family member or friend is depressed and talks about suicide, this is a warning sign. When someone opens up to you that he or she is contemplating suicide, do not be judgmental. Act with empathy and insist they seek help. Do not handle this alone. Call the police and a suicide prevention hotline for assistance. If you see something, say something—you just might save a life.

If you are depressed and feeling trapped, powerless, and alone, please realize you are not alone. People who care are standing by, ready to help you. There are suicide hotlines operating twenty-four hours a day, seven days a week. Call them! Never be afraid to reach out for help. Trained professionals are there for you; they chose that profession because they care.

GUILT PLAGUES THE survivors of a suicide victim. The question "What could I have done?" is played over and over in a survivor's consciousness. There is nothing you can do about the fact a loved one committed suicide. What you *can* do is try to understand why it happened and, through that understanding, strive to find inner peace with the passing. This journey isn't easy, and it may take a lifetime to achieve.

Jennifer told me she felt the spiritual presence of her deceased husband and wanted to make contact. I asked her not to tell me anything more prior to our interdimensional communication session.

"There is a man on your generational level coming through. He has an olive complexion, dark eyes—a real tough guy," I described.

"It's him! That's Lance!" Jennifer exclaimed.

I continued, "I'm seeing an image of a star, like a US Army logo…"

"Lance was in the Army Rangers," she told me.

"Your relationship was very, shall we say, passionate."

Jennifer's eyes softened. "He was my husband."

"The reason he's bringing this up is that this passion led to extremely heated arguments between the two of you—and one time in particular," I relayed.

Jennifer gazed at me and nodded.

"I'm also feeling a dizzy sensation. It seems that prior to his passing, he wasn't in his right mind—like his intellect was compromised by drugs or alcohol."

"He was drinking—and yes, we were arguing," Jennifer affirmed.

"Now I'm feeling an immense pain in my head. It's as if my skull is coming apart—and the cap of my skull is being blown off," I said, realizing what this meant.

Jennifer sat silently.

"He shot himself in the head," I perceived. "And he's so sorry. He keeps repeating that he didn't mean it! It wasn't your fault! There's nothing you could've done."

"When he got back from his last tour in Afghanistan, he began drinking a lot, and we'd argue. That night he was really drunk. He always kept guns in the house—I didn't like that." Jennifer wiped her eyes with a crumpled tissue.

She went on, "We were arguing. He picked up a hand gun—a Glock—and pointed it to his head and shouted, 'What do you want? Do you want me to blow my head off?'

"I begged him to not do that, and he said, 'It's not loaded.' But then he pulled the trigger—and—and..." Jennifer couldn't go on.

"But it did go off, didn't it?" I asked as the pain in my head intensified.

"He was trying to scare me—the clip wasn't in the gun, so he thought it wasn't loaded. But there was a bullet in the chamber!" Jennifer began to cry.

My heart went out to her.

"It was so horrible!" Jennifer's tears streamed from her eyes as her whole body shook. "I see it over and over in my head. It's my fault! I never should've argued with him when he was drunk."

"Jennifer, he keeps repeating how sorry he is and that he didn't mean it."

"Please ask him what I could've done differently."

"'Nothing,'" I relayed from Lance. "'I'm so sorry! I screwed up! And it wasn't your fault.'"

"I know he didn't mean it!" Jennifer exclaimed. "But—where is he? I don't know what to believe! Is he in the darkness? Is he alone? Is he suffering?"

"Two other spirits, a man and a woman, are coming through now. They seem like grandparents. The woman has some small objects in her hand—they look like little heart-shaped candies and she's telling me, 'They're the ones that taste like sweet chalk.'"

Jennifer looked up in surprise. "That's my grandmother! She used to give me those candies every Valentine's Day! And I'm embarrassed to say that when I was little, she caught me eating chalk!"

"I feel an overwhelming sense of peace from your grand-parents; they're in the Light. They're here to comfort you.

They're also working with Lance, reaching out to help him ascend to a higher frequency."

"Are you really sure he doesn't blame me?"

"Lance wants you to know it wasn't your fault—it was *his* fault. He loves you and wants to comfort you and apologize for what he did."

Lance's impulsive, irresponsible gesture resulted in a terrible tragedy. Although it wasn't her fault, Jennifer blamed herself. Sadly, she will carry that pain with her every day of her material world existence. After the reading, Jennifer confided that she was so guilt-ridden, she had considered suicide just to stop blaming herself. Instead, she chose to go to counseling. I agreed that therapy was the healthy way to address this problem and told her that continued treatment would be beneficial.

A mediumistic reading may be part of the healing process, yet it is only a part. Healing from guilt and coping with one's suicidal ideation require work and commitment. It is not something to bear alone.

Accepting the reality of suicide and finding inner peace with it is a long, arduous journey. Your constant companion on this journey may be guilt, yet guilt can be diminished through understanding. Sometimes this understanding will lead you to the realization that you were not responsible for the suicide. Seeking the assistance of trained professionals can help alleviate the burdens of guilt and grief.

WHAT ABOUT SOMEONE who uses suicide as a form of revenge? Some people take their own lives and do it to inflict the maximum amount of suffering and guilt upon others. Such an act has repercussions not just for the survivors in the material world but also for the spirit of the suicide victim on the Other Side.

Religions, in general, portray suicide as an act so heinous it requires the most severe of eternal punishments. As a child attending Catholic school, I was taught that anyone who commits suicide is condemned to hell. Even the usually tolerant Buddhists view suicide as an extremely negative act resulting in negative karmic repercussions.

God exists in spite of religion, not because of religion. Religion was created by finite human beings as an attempt to understand the infinity of God. In the positive sense, religions have been the vehicle to raise people's consciousness to a higher frequency. This has been necessary since humans have done a proficient job at inflicting suffering upon other humans. To avoid this, religions have created rules and guidelines.

Unfortunately, many religious rules and guidelines are based on fear in order to coerce people into conforming to particular behaviors. In a sense, they are forms of behavior modification. Behavior modification is based on rewards and punishment. Good behavior is rewarded; bad behavior is punished.

Suicide has been depicted by some religions as such an evil act that those committing suicide are condemned by

God. Ironically, such condemnation also inflicts tremendous suffering on the innocent survivors. It leaves them depressed and fearful that their loved one will never ascend to heaven. While the objective is a positive one designed to deter suicide, the result is often quite the opposite. It's the survivors who experience hell on earth. In this case, ironically, the road to hell *is* paved with good intentions.

On the other hand, religions offer many positive elements. They inspire faith in God and guide people to overcome the animalistic impulses of anger, bigotry, hatred, and violence, which have been the scourge of humanity. Religions can be the inspiration for people to rise above primeval aggressions and instead pursue the higher frequency of nonviolence, peace, forgiveness, understanding, and love. As His Holiness Pope John Paul II once wrote, "The essential usefulness of faith consists in the fact that, through faith, man achieves the good of his rational nature."

AFTER BEING DEFEATED in battle by the forces of Octavian Caesar and facing a humiliating execution, Antony and Cleopatra committed suicide. According to legend, the noble Mark Antony fell upon his own sword while his lover, Cleopatra, the exotic queen of Egypt, succumbed to the bite of a cobra.

Since ancient times, the list of famous people who have committed suicide is legion and, unfortunately, art and literature have often glorified the act. Suicide is anything but glorious. It leaves devastation in its wake, inflicting immense pain and suffering upon the survivors. Although a lot of planning and forethought may go into the decision to take one's own life, it may also require some form of permission to actually go through with it.

The proclivity to commit suicide appears to be increased in a family with a history of suicides. If a person contemplating suicide had a close friend or relative who committed suicide, then the chances increase that a depressed person may make that choice. While suicides may occur multiple times within a family, it does not mean it is a hereditary trait. It appears to be an imitated model of behavior. In other words, once the taboo is removed, it grants permission to one contemplating suicide to go through with it, especially if someone that person loved or admired had done it.

While on a tour of Denver, Colorado, I was invited by Diane Fresquez, the owner of For Heaven's Sake Bookstore and Metaphysical Center, to conduct a gallery reading. I was drawn to a woman seated next to her husband.

"A young man, it could be a son, is coming through—and it feels like he took his own life," I conveyed, looking to this woman.

She burst into tears. Lovingly, her husband held her while she sobbed.

"He seems to be with three other male spirits who were older than your son when they passed. All of them feel to me as if their lives ended abruptly," I said, realizing all of these men also had taken their lives.

Still crying, the woman spoke. "My son committed suicide when he was nineteen. When he was a little boy, my brother, his favorite uncle, hung himself. A few years later, my father took his life…and about a year before my son hung himself, his cousin, my sister's son, overdosed."

It was clear to see that this devastated young mother was drowning in a sea of sadness. A profound sense of sympathy filled the room as the wounds of grief reopened for many people as they, too, relived their own tragic losses.

The cry for healing was heard in heaven. I found myself moved to sing a song from the movie *The Lion King*.

The woman took a deep breath. "That was my son's favorite song! When he was six, he loved that movie!" she exclaimed, a smile transforming her sad face.

"How did you know that?" her husband asked me.

"I don't know it, but your son does. And he wants you to know how profoundly sorry he is for what he's done. These men who came with him are sorry for putting you and your family through such pain. They also want to apologize…and your son, in particular, is reaching out to you with compassion. He asks your forgiveness."

"Is he in hell for committing suicide?" the mother wondered, her smile now gone.

"He says no," I said, conveying the response. "He says, 'We are all children of God—and no parent could ever condemn a child to an eternity of suffering. God is the most loving parent of all.'"

My personal experiences as a medium have proved to me that God exists, heaven and the Other Side exist, souls are immortal, we can communicate with souls, and we will be reunited with our loved ones on the Other Side. I've also come to understand there is no hell, although there are multiple levels on the Other Side and reincarnation.

12

Reincarnation:
The Justice and Balance of God

One of the topics I'm asked about the most is reincarnation. It is difficult to discuss the afterlife and the Other Side without talking about it. In fact, every medium and near-death researcher I know believes in reincarnation.

It is especially important to touch upon this facet of eternal life in the discussion after suicide. Many fear their loved one who committed suicide has been condemned to hell. This concern of eternal damnation contradicts the evidence I've received from hundreds of spirits of those who have committed suicide. Suicide is such a complex behavior, with so many far-reaching repercussions, that despite what any religion may suggest, there is no "one size fits all" for what awaits the spirit of a person who commits suicide.

These spirits have explained that there is no hell, but that all suicides have to come back to the material world. Then again, we all return multiple times, so this is not unique to people who commit suicide. However, committing suicide does not cancel one's "debts" in this world; it appears to transfer them to another lifetime. This is not negative; it is balance. God gives us a lot of chances to get it right—and eventually, we will.

The Other Side has many levels, and your material world life has a direct correlation to the level you enter once you cross from this world to the next. Those who have led a self-centered existence and inflicted harm upon others do not immediately ascend into the higher frequencies of the Other Side; they transition to the lower levels. It appears some of these levels are either devoid of the Light or lacking a full connection to it, while those on the higher levels have a greater ability to perceive the Light.

We are all the children of God, and God's love is all-pervasive and forgiving. That is why a spirit is able to ascend from the lower levels into the higher frequencies of the Other Side. However, before that happens, they may have to return to the material world. For example, if the spirit who returns was a predator in his or her last life, he or she may very well be the victim in the next life. Reincarnation brings the universal balance of karma to us all.

Some religions attempt to suppress or condemn belief in reincarnation. This is ironic since reincarnation is deeply rooted in all of the major belief systems.

Nearly four thousand years ago, the Hindu sages of India taught about karma, the law of action and reaction. The actions of a person have a direct impact on whether that person reincarnates. Whatever you do comes back on you, so the objective is to not create more karma that requires rebirth. Hinduism acknowledges that suffering is an integral part of human life. As long as we are caught in the cycle of births and deaths, there is no escape from suffering. Aging, sickness, and death are the three afflictions of human life from which humankind finds no escape except by way of liberation from the material world and balancing out our karma so it is unnecessary for us to be reborn.

Three hundred years before Christ, Buddha taught that nothing in life is permanent and that life is an ongoing stream of consciousness, which transfers from one life to the next. Like Hindus, Buddhists also believe in karma—action or actions committed that leave an imprint on the consciousness. Actions can be positive or negative; it is for the person to choose. This stream of consciousness carries karmic imprints from previous lifetimes. The cycle of life, death, and rebirth will continue until there is no need to return to the material world. Unlike most other religions, Buddhists don't necessarily believe in God. They view Buddha as a supernatural teacher, not a supreme deity and judge. There is no need for judgment because karma is a natural law of balance.

Judaism teaches that when the Messiah, the king and savior of the Jewish people, comes to bring a world of peace and harmony, the dead will be resurrected. In Hebrew, this time is referred to as *olam ha-ba*, which means "the world to come." Resurrection is different from reincarnation. Resurrection means a person comes back to life, whereas reincarnation means a person is born into a new and different life.

However, among many Jewish mystical schools of thought and particularly among the Chasidic sect of Judaism, there is a belief that resurrection is a repeated process. The purpose of this repeated return to physical life is to resolve unfinished business—in other words, reincarnation.

Jesus taught that life is everlasting. Christians tend to think this means we are born and die, and everlasting life is a one-way ticket to heaven or hell with no return to the material world. However, there is another school of thought shared by many biblical scholars who believe Jesus spoke of reincarnation when he said the prophet Elijah had returned as John the Baptist as written in the Bible in Matthew 11:2–15, Matthew 17:10–13, and Mark 9:9–13.

This is not as farfetched as one might initially think. Many of the early Christian theologians also believed in reincarnation. The most famous was the philosopher Origen of Alexandria, who lived from AD 185 to AD 254. Origen rejected the notion of eternal damnation and taught that through multiple ages and the transmigration of spirits—reincarnation—all spirits will eventually be reunited with God.

Three hundred years after Origen and five centuries after Jesus's mission on earth, belief in reincarnation by Christians ground to a halt. In AD 553, during the reign of the Byzantine emperor Justinian, the Fifth Ecumenical Council in Constantinople was convened. The Christian Church issued a new version of the Bible and formally banned belief in reincarnation.

Over the following fifteen centuries, the Christian Bible was revised and edited several times. In the year AD 1054, religious and political squabbling between Rome and Constantinople caused the Christian world to split into two main segments, the Greek Orthodox and the Roman Catholic. Further divisions within both churches continued. By the seventeenth century, Martin Luther's teachings gave rise to Protestantism in Germany, not to mention a new version of the Bible. Shortly thereafter, Protestants broke away from the Roman Catholic Church. Religious divisions continue to this day, as do new translations and versions of the Bible.

This is not unique to Christianity. All religions have numerous sects, divisions, and doctrinal disputes. There are many paths to God, and that is why I believe that all faiths must be treated with respect. Too many people believe their way is the one and only way, and they often treat people who have different belief systems with contempt and prejudice. As Gandhi once stated, "We are all the children of God, so why do you

raise your hand against your brothers and sisters simply because they call God by a different name?"

WHY DON'T WE simply remember our previous lives?
Wouldn't that make our mystical journey of learning life lessons easier? The answer appears to lie with the human brain.
The brain is the filter between our eternal existence and a
material world existence. However, the spirit retains all of the
knowledge of our past lives.

Think of your spirit as a librarian who has read all of the
books in the library. She knows the characters in *The Iliad,*
War and Peace, The Great Gatsby, The Diary of Anne Frank, and
To Kill a Mockingbird. The characters in these books are totally
unaware of the characters in the other books. The warrior
Hector from *The Iliad* doesn't know the young, persecuted
Anne Frank, yet the common thread is that the librarian
knows them. She has experienced all of these characters and
knows their feelings, thoughts, personalities, and histories.

By analogy, while you are living one life, your spirit is
aware of the other lives. Your consciousness is limited to a
finite perception by your brain, which purposely makes you
unaware, at least temporarily, of the other characters you've
played throughout several lives.

A man from Ireland who didn't believe in reincarnation
contacted me for a reading. When I asked why, he replied, "I
can't bear the thought of never seeing her again."

"How so?" I needed to know more. "After you die and transition to the Other Side, you will be reunited with her."

"Not if she's reincarnated!" He seemed upset. "If I die and she has reincarnated, I won't see her in heaven because she won't be there. She'll be here as someone else!"

He raised an interesting question that I have been asked often. Many people worry their loved ones won't be there to greet them as they cross into the Light because the loved ones will have reincarnated. In the thousands of readings I've conducted, spirits always reassure loved ones that they will be there to greet a loved one who dies. What if the person you really want to see on the Other Side has reincarnated? What then?

Once again, when viewing the infinite through a finite set of eyes, we cannot possibly see the whole picture. Trying to grasp infinity with a finite brain is frustrating, to say the least.

We are energetic beings having a material world experience. Even though the material world is finite, our infinite spirit is energetically linked to God and, therefore, to the collective consciousness of the Other Side. Our brain is geared and programmed to temporarily limit our consciousness so we can have these material world experiences and learn from them. The Other Side is infinite and encompasses limitless dimensions. Our spirit in its pure energetic form is a multidimensional being, which means our perception and presence exist on several levels.

As multidimensional beings, even though our finite consciousness is having a material world existence, our spirit is still energetically linked to the collective consciousness of the Other Side. This means that even if someone has reincarnated, his or her spirit is still capable of interdimensional communication with a loved one in the material world about a previous lifetime.

Think of it this way: our spirit is the librarian who holds all of our records. When someone reincarnates, spirit communication with that person's spirit is possible. For example, Anne Frank dies and reincarnates as Scout from *To Kill a Mockingbird*. Anne's cousin, Martha, wants to communicate with Anne's spirit, so she visits a medium. Even though Anne has reincarnated as Scout, the spirit is still able to communicate with Martha since the spirit retains the memories and personality of Anne Frank. Once again, the brain is the arbiter between our material world experience and our infinite consciousness. There is one consciousness, and within that consciousness are multiple dimensions.

Throughout the procession of lifetimes we experience, we change gender, race, religion, ethnicity, sexual orientation, and physical capabilities. As spirits do not possess these characteristics, the reason is to experience the full gamut of life in this material world dimension.

The brain may be the filter that prevents us from total recall of previous incarnations; however, there is a way around that filter. Past-life regression therapy uses hypnosis to bring a person back before their birth to recall prior lifetimes.

I've observed past-life regression hypnotherapy sessions. While very impressive, I haven't seen evidence to substantiate this type of therapy, particularly when the lifetime recalled is centuries ago and there is no way to verify the accuracy of the information recalled by the subject. Evidential mediumship requires facts to be brought out that will verify what a spirit presents. However, I cannot dismiss past-life regression therapy because I've also seen how revisiting a past life can help to alleviate emotional stress occurring during a current lifetime.

Evidence to support reincarnation may exist. There are actual case studies of people who have recalled prior lifetimes where the evidence they were able to present could be verified.

The most thoroughly researched investigation of reincarnation in modern history occurred in India during the 1930s. Shanti Devi was born in 1926 in Delhi, India. Shortly after her fourth birthday, she informed her parents, "This isn't my real home. I have a husband and son in the city of Mathura. I must return to them!" Her parents were shocked.

This was just the beginning. She began to "recall" extremely intricate details of her previous life, including the address of her former home. She said her real name was Lugdi Devi; her husband was Kedarnath, a cloth merchant in Mathura; and she died shortly after giving birth to her son.

Using the information provided by Shanti, the headmaster of her school wrote a letter to the address Shanti said was her previous home. He was shocked when he received a reply from Kedarnath indicating his young wife had died a few years earlier after childbirth, exactly as Shanti had described.

News of this reached the Indian government, which enlisted Mahatma Gandhi to set up a commission to investigate Shanti Devi's claims of reincarnation. A team of researchers was assembled to test her and guarantee that she was not receiving information from any outside source.

The team took Shanti by train to Mathura, some ninety miles from Delhi. When they arrived, Shanti, without any guidance, led the research team to what she described as her previous home. She explained in accurate detail what the house used to look like when she lived there.

As part of the test, Shanti was introduced to an actor posing as her husband. The real Kedarnath stood next to the actor and was introduced as his brother. Shanti pointed at Kedarnath and said, "No, he is not my husband's brother. He is my husband."

She then revealed very delicate personal details no one outside the family could have known. These included extramarital affairs of family members and that, in her previous incarnation as Lugdi, she had painful arthritis, which made sexual relations with Kedarnath difficult.

The commission's report concluded Shanti Devi was the reincarnation of Lugdi Devi. Award-winning Swedish journalist Sture Lonnerstrand spent months with Shanti to document this investigation in great detail. Shanti was interviewed several times throughout her life, the last interview only four days before her death on December 27, 1987.

Louise Eady was born into a gentile family in Edwardian England in 1904. When she was three years old, she was seriously injured in a fall and pronounced dead. Miraculously, she returned to life, and her family was overjoyed—until she began to talk about her previous life in ancient Egypt during the reign of Pharaoh Seti I, three thousand years earlier.

During a visit with her family to the British Museum, young Louise saw a photograph of the Temple of Seti I in Abydos and exclaimed, "There is my home! But where are the trees?" Naturally, her proper English family thought her mad. Her father sent her to a psychiatrist to rectify these delusions. She endured years of therapy but remained adamant about her prior life.

Finally she'd had enough of her family's rejection of her beliefs. As a young woman, she left England for Egypt to work with famed Egyptologist Selim Hassan at the Great Pyramids in Giza. She rapidly learned to read, write, and decipher ancient Egyptian hieroglyphic text. The experts were amazed at her grasp of this extremely complex language.

She took the name Om-Seti (Seti's mother) and left Giza to work on an excavation of the Temple of Seti I near Abydos. She explained to the archaeological team that, in a prior life, she was a priestess at the Temple of Seti I and her name had been Bentreshyt.

The archaeologists humored her claim that a garden with trees once existed next to the Temple of Seti and that a tunnel ran underneath the northern section of the temple. However, their attitudes changed when the excavation unearthed both the remains of a garden and the tunnel—exactly where she said they were.

Om–Seti gained great popularity among the local Egyptians and became something of a celebrity. Her knowledge and understanding of ancient Egypt during the time of Pharaoh Seti I was legendary. Tourists flocked to the region for her lectures and tours. She donated all the money she raised to the poor until her death in 1981. Her only request was to be buried near the Temple of Seti I.

She was featured in many articles and television documentaries about ancient Egypt and reincarnation. During one interview, she said a lot of people who believe they are reincarnated come to Egypt hoping to reconnect with a prior life. While people may identify with a particular period of history from a prior life, not everyone was a king or queen. Om–Seti once joked, "You have no idea how many Cleopatras I've met."

The stigma against belief in reincarnation appears to be waning in the Western world. As more cases of reincarnation are documented, it is now discussed openly. Perhaps you feel you've lived before. Maybe you've had a dream of a previous life, feel a connection with a particular historical period, or met someone for the first time and feel you've known each other before.

There will come a time when all of us will die; nothing can change that. The issue, though, isn't dying; the issue is being reborn. Failure to follow the path of Light in the material world ensures that there is no escaping reincarnation, the justice and balance created by God. In karma, as in physics, for every action, there is an equal and opposite reaction.

All of the great spiritual teachers have inspired us to commit positive actions and avoid the negative. The objective of the journey of the spirit is to ascend to the higher frequencies of the Other Side and not return.

Until then, we must experience the lessons, challenges, and pain of living in the material world.

13

The Death of a Child
and the Other Side

D*eath leaves a heartache no one can heal; love leaves a memory no one can steal* is etched on a headstone in an ancient Irish cemetery. It may be the truest statement about coping with loss, particularly when it comes to the death of a child.

A child's death is the epitome of injustice because the natural order of life has been distorted. Children are supposed to outlive their parents.

Losing a child begins a lifetime bereavement process. Unfortunately, grief has no expiration date, and everyone progresses through it at an individual pace. Everyone manifests grief in his or her own way. It is normal to feel anger, despair, guilt, and sadness at the death of a child. Often parents feel guilty, feeling that they could have in some way prevented it. This is true even though the vast majority of the time, the parent is in no way responsible for the child's death.

Comforting a parent who has lost a child is difficult. It doesn't matter if the child was a fetus or a senior citizen, the loss is excruciating. If you are trying to comfort a grieving parent, please avoid saying things like "you can always have another baby" or "you have other children" or "she's in a better place" or "it's all part of God's plan." While these sentiments may be made with the best of intentions, they will most likely have the opposite effect.

Each person is unique, and just because parents have or can have other children, it's impossible to replace the unique person who died. Saying someone's child is in a better place and it's part of God's plan will likely infuriate a grieving parent. Parents do not want to hear that the death of their child was part of a plan—or that their child is somehow better off without them.

If you have lost a child and have other children, it's extremely important to make sure the surviving siblings are given proper emotional support. Children are very sensitive and observe the devastation death brings. Unlike adults, children lack the maturity and skill set to cope with the enormity of the loss. Older children may be able comprehend the concept of death, while younger children may not. In either case, death is terrifying to a child.

When a family member dies, a surviving child needs honesty, support, and a stable home life. A child needs to know that he or she is loved and that it is all right to grieve, be sad, and cry. Both children and adults need to talk about their feelings when it comes to death and have the opportunity to express their feelings, pain, depression, and anger.

Earlier in the book, I indicated that in my practice as a criminal defense attorney I've seen how grief leads to crime and crime leads to grief. Several of my clients turned to a life of crime because of unresolved grief issues from childhood. Many children aren't given the opportunity to properly cope with loss. "Get over it" or "don't think about it" do not help. Unresolved grief will surface in negative ways such as drug and alcohol addiction, impulsive behaviors, and violence. Ultimately, the child may transform into a criminal who inflicts suffering upon others.

Comforting your surviving child or children by helping them cope with death is a daunting challenge, yet it is a challenge you must face. Letting a child express his or her feelings is crucial to the journey through grief. When you talk to children about death, you will learn what they know and don't know about death. You will begin to understand their fears and can help to provide information and understanding, which leads to acceptance. It is through acceptance of the reality of the death that both parent and child can eventually come to the objective of the journey through grief, which is inner peace.

Inner peace does not mean either parent or child will ever fully recover from a death in the family. What it means is that emotional stability will return and a new normal will emerge. The new normal does not include the physical presence of the child who died. The new normal is an acknowledgment that change is inevitable in life. Although change isn't always painful, it often is, and one must learn to manage life's difficulties.

To cope with loss, you must let go of the sorrow caused by the death but hold on to the love for the one who has passed. This may help you recover from the initial shock caused by death. Recovering from the trauma imposed by death takes much longer. It requires a commitment to healing, which can take years.

Holding on to the love for the person who died is necessary for this healing. With death, a relationship transforms from one of a physical nature to one of a spiritual nature. That realization is essential to understanding that, although the physical existence has ended, the spiritual existence of the person continues.

Talking about the death with your family members, both adults and children, is another key to healing. Open and frank discussion leads to expression of fear and pain that need to be released so healing can occur. Talking may not resolve all of the pain arising from death, but it is a critical element of the healing process.

Talking may require more than just conversations with loved ones here in the material world. Sometimes, as part of the healing process, it is beneficial to have a conversation with your loved one on the Other Side.

The spirit of a person preexists the body and lives on after the physical death of the body. During interdimensional communication, the spirit usually projects an image of his or her appearance prior to passing when initially making contact. This is part of a process to establish the identity of the spirit.

This is also part of the communication process. Spirits transmit waves of frequency to the medium, and each progressive wave presents another piece of evidence, which becomes more detailed. Spirits will convey several pieces of evidence such as a personality profile, likes and dislikes, and shared memories between the client and the spirit when they were living in the material world.

Spirits of unborn children are intelligent, sentient, and fully capable of interdimensional communication. Contact with these spirits is a bit different since there are no shared experiences with the parents. However, they are still conscious of what is happening in the material world.

While meditating prior to a reading for Dana and Paul, I briefly felt the presence of a male child. This isn't unusual because spirits know we're going to engage in interdimensional communication, so they often appear prior to a reading.

Spirits love to communicate with us, and many times it seems they're even more excited about communicating with us than we are with them.

As soon as the session began, I saw a bright and radiant light that looked like a little star. I perceive unborn children as a star of light because a physical description of them as a child wouldn't make sense. It may also have to do with the fact they are untainted by a material world life and exist as pure spiritual energy. This star is a beautiful image, although it can bring immense sadness to the parents, who never got to see this child alive.

"There's the spirit of a baby—a boy. Does this make sense to you?" I asked.

"No, we never had a boy," Paul replied. Dana looked stunned.

"We didn't…but I did," Dana admitted softly.

Now it was Paul who looked stunned.

"Years ago, I…lost a child. I didn't know what the sex was, but somehow I always thought it was a boy."

Gently, Paul took her hand. "It's okay, honey."

"I'm seeing an image of Archangel Michael. Does that image have meaning for either of you?" I looked first to Dana and then at Paul.

"Yes, if it was a boy, I planned to name him Michael," Dana shared.

Absolve, I heard the spirit say. "His message is one of absolution."

"What does that mean?" Dana asked.

"It means he forgives you. He doesn't want you to feel bad. He's felt your pain and regret over all these years," I conveyed.

"What happened?" Paul asked, looking at Dana.

"I—I—had an abortion." Dana looked away from Paul.

"You did what!" Paul's voice was angry.

"Paul!" I interjected. "I know this is sensitive, but give her a chance! Besides, this boy is reaching out to forgive her."

"I've always regretted it," Dana wept. "I was so young… and I was with the wrong man. I hoped I could make a go of things, but when I found out…"

"Found out what?" Paul asked, his temper subsiding.

"There was something wrong with the baby. Both the father and I tested positive for a rare genetic disorder called cobalamin C deficiency. It's a disorder that impairs the body's ability to process protein, and it's very serious. It can result in birth defects and all kinds of problems. I was so afraid…and I've regretted it ever since."

"Oh, honey—I'm so sorry," Paul cried, taking Dana in his arms.

More was coming to me. "Michael—I'm going to refer to him by that name—he has a message," I told Dana.

"Please tell me what Michael wants me to know," Dana implored.

"He says don't worry. He'll come into this world when it is his time. That's what he wants you to know. He says he feels your pain and wants you to be free of it."

"It's nice of you to say that for our benefit," Paul said to me.

"Now Michael is showing me a radio and the number 97." I looked to both of them for a response.

"For real?" Paul exclaimed as he and Dana shot each other surprised glances.

"Our favorite radio station is 97.4! Now, how on earth does Michael know that?" Dana asked.

I continued to relay what I was seeing. "He's showing me the image of an Easter lily. This appears to be a multiple-meaning message—a message with more than one level of significance."

"I had the abortion about a week before Easter, and my sister gave me a bracelet with an Easter lily engraved on it as a memorial. She knew how upset I was." Dana began to weep again.

I looked at Dana to give her Michael's final message. "Michael forgives you. He knows what you've been through and he's aware of what is going on in your life. Most importantly, he loves you."

ALEX AND HIS wife, Tara, contacted me for a reading over the telephone.

"A younger male—like a son—is coming through," I told them.

"Yes, go on," Alex said, anxious to hear more.

"He liked Jell-O *a lot*," I described.

"That's him!" Tara exclaimed. "Our son loved Jell-O!"

I continued, "He had an incredible mind...he was extremely intelligent."

"Yes, he did," Alex agreed.

"His passing was quick. I see a mirror and tile—it seems he was in a bathroom."

"We found his body in the bathroom," his father said softly.

"I feel dizzy—like there's a spinning sensation in my head," I conveyed. "I associate this with a mental disruption prior to passing. I'm seeing pills, little white pills, so—I..."

"Go on, you can say it." Tara knew what was coming.

"This is what I normally associate with a drug overdose— although he doesn't seem like a drug addict. He seemed so happy in his life. I'm not getting any of the depression that I usually get with people who had drug or alcohol problems," I told them.

"Our son died of an interaction between two different prescription drugs," Alex explained. "He wasn't a drug addict. We've brought a wrongful death lawsuit against his doctor and the pharmaceutical company. Our son should not have died."

"I'm seeing the number 17! It appears to be extremely important; does that number mean anything to either of you?" I asked.

"No...he wasn't seventeen, he was twenty-seven years old," Tara said tentatively.

"I know what 17 means," Alex interjected. "It has been exactly seventeen months since my son died—seventeen months to this day. I count the days since he died."

"R—I'm getting an R sound in his name," I conveyed.

"The R is for Roy. His name was Roy." Alex began to weep.

Roy's spirit continued to relay a lot of details about his life and his passing. He was an extremely popular schoolteacher, and his funeral service had been standing room only. His parents were extremely appreciative about making this contact with their son. However, at the end of the reading, something happened that I did not expect.

Alex explained he was the chief executive officer of a large and well-known corporation.

"Thank you for entrusting me to facilitate contact with your son," I replied.

Alex explained that he would be coming to Florida on business. He wanted to meet with me to discuss something important.

The next month, I met Alex and his assistant at a restaurant for dinner. He had a very down-to-earth and approachable manner. I could see why he was so well known and popular.

After dinner, he took out his smartphone and said, "There's something important you need to see."

He showed photos he'd taken on his phone. I noticed his assistant's demeanor stiffen.

"Look! Here is a picture of my wife in our living room. Do you see it?"

"Your wife is a beautiful woman," I complimented.

"No! Do you see it?"

"See what?" I asked, completely confused.

"Here, look—on the wall behind my wife. Do you see the face in the plaster on the wall?"

"Uh, okay," I responded, not really sure what I was supposed to be seeing.

He went on, "How about this one? Here's a picture of my wife sitting on the sofa. Can you see it here—can you see the spirit's face in the sofa?"

I've worked with several professionals in both the United States and Great Britain who specialize in the study of spectral phenomena. I've seen thousands of photographs of alleged images of spirits captured on both film and in digital format. What I saw on his smartphone didn't appear to be the image of a spirit.

"Can't you see it? It's my son. His face is in the wall—it's in the fabric of the sofa! He's with us!" Alex exclaimed as his assistant looked away, closing her eyes.

I reached across the table and took the smartphone from him.

"Alex, listen to me. Your son is not in your wall or in your sofa. Your son is dead," I told him. The assistant appeared shocked that I'd addressed him in that manner.

Alex's eyes locked on mine. "But you…you, of all people, should understand," he pleaded. I saw before me not a powerful business executive but an anguished father devastated by the loss of his son.

"Alex, I do understand, but what you must understand is that your son, Roy, is not in these photos...he is not in your wall and he is not in your couch."

Alex stared at me.

"Roy is an immortal living spirit. That is true. He does visit you, and he's energetically connected to you and to your family," I explained as gently as I could.

Alex's eyes began to water.

"You're clinging to the physical. You want your son with you so much that you would do anything to have him here." I could feel his pain.

"It's true!" Alex said, tears streaming from his eyes. "I miss him so much—if only he could come back to me."

"He does come to you spiritually, but you have to let go of the attachment to the physical. That part of his existence has ended. He's an immortal living spirit, and you have to accept that," I implored.

Alex's assistant paid the check and suggested we call it a night.

As we said our goodbyes in the parking lot, the persona of the executive returned as he said, "No one talks to me like that. You're very bold—but I appreciate that."

"Thanks," I said, wondering if I'd overstepped my bounds.

As Alex went to get his car, the assistant whispered to me, "Thank God you said that to him. His son's death has taken such a toll on him. I've been afraid he'd show those photos to the wrong people. Big business can be vicious, and his enemies would circle around that like sharks."

Nearly two months later, Alex's wife, Tara, called me.

"Mr. Anthony, I want to thank you. I don't know what you did or what you said to Alex, but he's a changed man. He's moving forward with his life. I think he's finally laid our son to rest."

Death is the great equalizer and something we must all cope with at some point in our lives. It doesn't matter how much education, position, or money you have; all losses are devastating. The death of a child, though, stands apart. It doesn't matter if your child is an infant or an adult; losing a child is devastating.

A COMMUNITY SERVICE organization asked me to conduct a presentation about the several US presidents who have consulted psychic advisers. About a hundred people attended this event, and at the conclusion of my presentation I was asked to conduct a gallery reading. Drawn to an attractive middle-aged woman, I asked her to stand and she obliged.

"There's a younger female coming through who feels like a daughter. Her passing was a long, slow decline. I feel a draining sensation throughout my entire body. This condition caused her to become very thin prior to passing," I conveyed.

"She died of leukemia," the woman confided.

"It seems she liked the color purple," I said.

The woman nodded. "A few months before she died, my daughter asked to have her room painted purple."

"She is showing me a piece of paper like a prayer card. It's about the size of an index card…like the ones sometimes used at memorial services. Your daughter seems to indicate that this brings you comfort."

"Two days after my daughter died, I found this by her bed," the woman said, gently removing a small sheet of paper from her purse for me to see. "She wrote this for me to find." Her hands were trembling as she held the precious paper gingerly. After a short pause, she asked, "May I read it?"

The room became very still. "Of course," I replied.

Perhaps God is a poet,
Who writes with words of flesh and bone and leaf and flower.
Every hour of every day words pour out of the poet's heart.
And every word is beautiful and true and worth telling.
And when each poem is perfect,
And there is no more which ought to be said,
The poet gently takes the words back into his heart
Where they are safe forever…
And then begins again.

When she had finished reading her daughter's poem, there wasn't a dry eye in the room.

14

Animals and Unconditional Love from Heaven

S andhill cranes mate for life. Standing nearly five feet tall, these gray-colored birds sport a bright red patch atop their heads and are one of the most majestic species of birds that grace the state of Florida. With an immense wingspan, they look more suited to a scene in *Jurassic Park* than to a field or golf course in Florida.

One afternoon, I was driving by a golf course near my office when I saw two sandhill cranes striding across the road. Normally, traffic stops for these splendid creatures; however, a pickup truck driven by a young man swerved toward one of the cranes, killing it. The driver of the pickup truck appeared to be laughing and drove away as if he'd done nothing wrong.

I was shocked and pulled over. What I witnessed was profound. The surviving sandhill crane stood over the carcass of its mate making a loud warbling sound, the likes of which I'd never heard before. It seemed the surviving bird was crying. This tragic event saddened me, and I tried to rationalize the bird's behavior as a genetically encoded response...but was it?

The next day on my way to the office, I observed the sandhill crane still there, standing sentinel over the body of its mate. For the next two weeks, the crane remained in the same spot by the road where its life partner had died. Was this bird actually grieving? Was the sandhill crane feeling the pain that only the death of a loved one can inflict?

LAWRENCE ANTHONY WAS a conservationist who dedicated his life to saving elephants. Whether it was liberating elephants from abuse in circuses or preventing rogue elephants from being shot, Lawrence Anthony came to the rescue. In the mid-1990s, Anthony bought the 5,000-acre Thula Thula Reserve in South Africa as a refuge for wild animals, notably elephants. He and his wife lived in a house on the reserve to ensure it remained an environment where these noble beings would be able to live in their native habitat and be safe from poachers.

Anthony worked tirelessly to save elephants worldwide. His efforts gained international recognition in 2003 for his rescue work at the Baghdad Zoo in the aftermath of the US invasion. When Anthony learned of elephants abandoned in Baghdad, he knew he had to act and immediately departed for Iraq. He was appalled when he found the elephants starving.

If Anthony was to save these elephants, he knew he had to act quickly, but he needed help. He also understood that compassion truly brings out the best in humans. Iraqi citizens and US soldiers alike answered Anthony's plea for help. Setting aside their differences, they banded together and helped him save the lives of the stranded elephants.

In March 2012, Anthony died suddenly from a heart attack at his home in South Africa at the Thula Thula Reserve. Two days after his death, something profound occurred. Wild elephants marching slowly and in single-file formation began to arrive at his house. This prolific procession of pachyderms continued for twelve hours until a herd of thirty-one elephants surrounded the Anthony home.

For two days and nights, without eating, the herd stood vigil outside Lawrence Anthony's home. Experts were dumbfounded, onlookers astonished. Anthony's widow, Francoise, was deeply touched. It appeared these creatures were honoring a friend who had shown mercy and compassion to their species. When the elephants had finished paying their respects, the herd dispersed and returned to the wild. In their wake, a question remained: how did they know?

UNITED STATES SUPREME court justice Oliver Wendell Holmes said, "Even a dog knows the difference between being kicked and being stumbled over." While that may be true, animals understand a lot more than we think they do. Observations of complex social structures and behaviors of all types of animals from dolphins to elephants indicate they are anything but dumb. Animals merely manifest intelligence differently than humans do.

Several species engage in behaviors that are considered intelligent. For example, some of them—including birds, sea otters, elephants, and apes—use tools. By definition, a tool is a physical item used to achieve a designated purpose. Dr. Jane Goodall was one of the first experts in primate behavior to observe chimpanzees modifying twigs to help them catch ants for food. This means chimps are not only using tools but creating them.

Dr. Goodall's pioneering research into the study of chimpanzee behavior revealed remarkable similarities between humans and chimpanzees. Goodall once said, "I wanted to talk to the animals like Dr. Doolittle." She discovered that interspecies communication is possible when it is understood how a species conveys information. In the case of chimpanzees, they communicate much like humans do. They kiss, hug, hold hands, pat each other on the back, and even tickle each other.

Chimpanzees also use facial expressions and even have temper tantrums.

Interspecies communication is also possible from the Other Side. Any being capable of the emotion of love is capable of spirit communication. Love is an emotion that transcends species, which is why interspecies interdimensional communication is similar to interdimensional communication with human spirits.

Practically every medium I've worked with has conducted readings for people whose loved ones in spirit did not speak English. Despite this obstacle, the spirit was fully capable of transmitting coherent and relevant messages through the medium. The reason for this is that spirits don't speak English, Spanish, Japanese, or any other human language. Rather, spirits transmit intelligence in the form of energetic vibration. Through this means of communication, the differences in cultures and even species are eliminated. Whether human or animal, once freed from the confines of a finite existence, a spirit communicates through vibrating waves of frequency that contain concepts, images, sensations, and emotions. These waves of frequency emitted by the spirit interface with the medium's energy and are translated into recognizable information based on the memories, feelings, and cultural references housed in the medium's brain.

Pets are tamed animals that have been incorporated into a human environment. Dogs, cats, birds, and horses are the ones most often living with us. They also have the strongest emotional bonds to humans. While we both may experience love, we experience the material world in different ways. Animals capable of the emotion of love, like dogs and cats, love unconditionally. Unconditional love is absolute and without doubt or question. There is no equivocation of one's feelings or the subtleties and nuances often complicating human relationships.

Love is truly a gift from God, and true love is a two-way street. The wonderful thing about love is that it transcends physical death. When we grieve for a loved one, human or animal, we emit a frequency beacon to that spirit—and the spirit will reach out to comfort us.

CHERI HART IS the owner of Aquarian Dreams Bookstore and Metaphysical Center in Florida. She invited me to conduct a presentation about the use of spirit contact as a tool in healing from grief. As part of the presentation, I conducted a gallery reading and was drawn to Stacey.

The spirits of her mother, father, and brother made contact. During the reading, it was revealed from the Other Side that Stacey's brother had died in his swimming pool of a heart attack.

"I see the three members of your family together," I described. "They're in the Light and looking young, healthy, and beautiful."

Tears streamed down Stacey's face.

"Your brother's death exacerbated your mother's condition. Did she die of a stroke? I see her going blind in one eye." I looked to Stacey for a response.

"His death was too much for my mother—she died of a stroke two weeks after my brother died of a heart attack." Stacey wept as she spoke.

"As painful as that information may be, I'm seeing three very happy, very beautiful people together in this incredible white Light and…" I paused, surprised by another spiritual energy that literally jumped into the middle of the message.

"Who had the cat?" I asked.

"My cat just died!" Stacey exclaimed, wiping her eyes.

"Well, there's a cat there with your family."

"Awww!" the crowd murmured collectively.

"That has to be Hercules! He was fifteen years old…he was my baby," Stacey shared.

"I hear him purring really loudly," I said, imitating the cat's purr. Hercules's love and joy positively resonated through me.

"Hercules just died last week! I miss him so much. Is he okay?"

"Well, he's in heaven! It's hard to be more okay than that!" I joked, feeling the mood of Stacey and the crowd lifted because of the gregarious and loving presence of Hercules the cat.

Stacey was mourning her family as well as her pet. She came from a family rich in love. Her loved ones, human and feline, reached out to comfort her. Stacey understood what a blessing it was to have had such a loving and close-knit family. Not all people are so blessed. For many, the only loving relationship in their lives is with a pet, and that relationship means everything to that person.

WHILE VISITING RHODE Island, I was facilitating a discussion about grief when an elderly woman raised her hand. "Please, Mark, can you make contact with my dog?"

A number of people in the crowd suppressed chuckles, as if this woman's grief over the loss of her beloved pet was somehow silly.

"I see a dog about the size of a Yorkshire terrier with teeth missing that made his tongue hang out—kind of gave him a goofy expression," I described.

"That's Pepper!" the woman said, putting her hand to her mouth.

"Your dog—Pepper—wants to acknowledge that you were with him when he died," I conveyed.

"Yes, I was."

"Now I'm experiencing dizziness and a gasping sensation," I explained. "It appears that it was a struggle for Pepper to breathe…and then he just let go," I explained.

"I couldn't do it—I couldn't have him put to sleep! Was I wrong?" she wondered with a sad expression.

"No. He does not want you to feel bad. He is showering you with love and affection. In fact, this animal loved you more than you can even imagine. Pepper is showing me how he looked up into your eyes at the moment of his death," I conveyed.

Her tear-filled eyes indicated a confirmation.

"But there's more! It's uncanny…this dog wants you to know that, as far as he felt, his death could not have been happier! Looking up into the face of the being he admired more than anything…" I paused. "I—I can only explain this as dying while looking into the face of love itself."

Members of the audience were no longer marginalizing this woman's pain. They were as touched as I was by this immense expression of love and devotion from the spirit of Pepper the Yorkshire terrier.

"And now another entity is coming forward," I told the woman. "This one is very different."

The woman looked up through her tears. "What—who is it?"

"A white- and ginger-colored cat is coming through…and I'm also seeing an image from *Peter Pan*—it's Tinkerbell!" I said, noticing the woman's surprise.

"Tinkerbell!" she exclaimed. "She was my first kitty when I was a little girl. That was almost sixty years ago!"

I continued, "Tinkerbell certainly is not going to be upstaged by a dog—and wow! Does this cat have some personality…"

"Yes, she did!" the woman confirmed. The mood in the room seemed to lighten.

"This cat was very fastidious. In fact, you might say she was downright picky," I described.

The woman blushed.

"Oh gosh!" I said, hearing more of the cat's message.

"What? What does Tinkerbell want me to know?"

"She's so grateful for the way you cleaned her litter box. She would only use a clean box and wouldn't use it if poop were in it. She appreciated that," I relayed, my face turning beet red.

The entire room broke out into laughter.

"That was Tinkerbell!" she replied. "She was so fussy! She had to have clean kitty litter, and if she didn't, she'd let us know by going somewhere else."

"Well," I said with relief. "I don't think I can trump kitty litter, so I'll leave that with you!"

Children love pets deeply and unconditionally. Even though Tinkerbell the cat had died decades earlier, the woman carried that pain with her into adulthood. In numerous ways, pets become members of the family. It is natural to go through profound grief at the loss of a pet, and this is particularly true for children. For many children, the death of a pet is the child's first experience with death. A pet's death is emotionally troubling and terrifying for the child. When a pet dies, a child realizes that other pets and even people the child loves will die as well.

This is why it is essential to help your child deal with the loss of a pet. Since death does not spare anyone, we can try to help a child cope with it. Adults have the benefit of life experience, maturity, and an emotional skill set, enabling a better understanding of death. It is best to encourage a child's expression of grief. Even if the pet was "just a frog" or "only a goldfish," respect for your child's feelings and permission to mourn the pet may help in the coping process, and this can have a very significant effect on your child's emotional development.

ALL ANIMALS WE love are special. However, some animals play a particularly significant role in the life of humans. Service animals, usually dogs such as seeing-eye dogs or police dogs, are not only loyal friends but friends that others' lives depend upon. This was never made clearer to me than during a gallery reading on Veteran's Day, 11/11/11, at Barnes and Noble in Philadelphia.

"A spirit would like to communicate with you," I said, drawn to Trevor, a gentleman seated in the front row. He was an intense and serious-looking man.

"Yes, sir," he replied.

"I'm feeling panting...heaving and rapid breathing. Wait! This doesn't feel like a human spirit," I told him.

"It's okay—go ahead." The man stared at me.

"This is a dog. A male dog—a very large dog—like a German shepherd," I described.

"Yes, he was a German shepherd," Trevor acknowledged.

Trevor's wife, who was seated next to him, took his hand.

"Something about the whistle—there was a special whistle." I watched for a response.

The audience listened as Trevor made an unusual whistling sound. "That was our special signal."

"He says he made a growling sound like snoring when he slept, " I conveyed. The link with this spirit intensified.

"Ajax—that's his name—had a deviated air passage in one of his nostrils, and he snored really loudly!" Trevor said with a smile.

"Ajax," I conveyed, "is showing me what looks like a red pillow."

"It was actually a red towel," Trevor explained. "Ajax used to drool. When he was in the back seat, he rested his head on the center console next to me. I had this red towel for him to put his jaw on so the drool wouldn't get all over the leather."

"He's showing me something different now," I relayed. "And this is intense! It's night—3 AM. At 3 AM he reacted faster than anyone else could have."

Trevor tensed. "I'm a police officer. Ajax was my canine partner—and one night a murder suspect was on the loose."

The large crowed listened intently.

"Several officers pursued the suspect, who ditched his car and then fled on foot into a wooded area," Trevor reported.

"Did this occur at 3 AM?" I asked.

"Yes," Trevor confirmed, gripping the arms of his chair. "We were pursuing the suspect into the woods, and I got separated from Ajax and the rest of the cops. I found myself alone and it was really dark…"

Complete silence engulfed the room.

"I had my gun out and a flashlight in my left hand. The woods were dense, and I figured the trail went cold. Suddenly, this guy—the killer, who was hiding behind a tree—jumped me! He took me completely by surprise..."

The audience sat transfixed.

"He hit me hard, and I went down. My gun fell to the ground. He was a big guy—really strong—and he pinned me down..."

Several gasps were heard as Trevor continued, "He held me by the throat with his left hand, and then in the moonlight I saw this flash of metal in his right. A huge knife was plunging straight at my chest and I thought *I'm going to die!*"

No one in the room said a word.

"Then, out of nowhere, a shadow flew over me."

Silence filled the large room. The crowd was on the edge of their seats.

"It was Ajax! Ajax intercepted the knife—grabbed the guy's right arm in his jaws and pulled him off of me."

"And what happened next?" I couldn't contain myself.

"Ajax ripped the guy up pretty bad! The guy was screaming his head off!"

"Good!" a woman in the row behind him exclaimed.

"I rolled away from Ajax and the guy and fumbled on the ground until I found my weapon—my gun. I yelled 'freeze!' and aimed it at his head. Even with all the screaming and Ajax growling, I could hear the other cops calling to me. They were still minutes away, but Ajax—he reacted faster than any person could have. He saved my life!" The memory proved too much for Trevor, and he broke down and sobbed.

I was impressed at how clearly Ajax communicated that this incident occurred at 3 AM. Then Ajax pressed me to deliver a final message.

"Prior to passing, Ajax apparently was in excruciating pain," I described. "His hip and legs hurt so much, he could barely move."

Trevor nodded solemnly.

I added, "He forgives you for putting him down. He knows you did this out of love for him—and to stop his suffering."

"He was the best friend I ever had. He was with me eighteen years…that dog just seemed to know what I was thinking—he could sense my moods—and he always knew how to make me feel better. Putting him down was the hardest thing I've ever done." Still weeping, Trevor covered his face with both hands.

I concluded the readings and signed books for attendees. After nearly an hour the crowd thinned, yet Trevor remained behind. Before he left, he shook my hand and said, "Ajax was always waiting for me at the door when I came home. And now I know he'll be waiting for me when I go home."

Inlightenment:
Embracing the Inner Light

My travels through Japan and Thailand to study Buddhism were life-enriching experiences, but after touring the Far East it was time to return home. My flight from Bangkok to New York City took over eighteen hours. When I landed at Kennedy International Airport, I had to catch a taxi to Newark Airport for the last leg of my trip back to Florida. Needless to say, it was a long and exhausting day.

When I stepped out of the terminal at Kennedy International Airport, several taxi drivers were arguing with each other about who was going to get my fare. One of them shoved the others aside, grabbed my bags, and said, "You! Come with me!"

He flung my suitcases into the trunk of his taxi. I had little choice but to follow and jump in the back seat before he sped off. He was quite animated and engaging as he drove, telling me his name was Hussein and he was from Egypt. His big, expressive green eyes glared frequently at me in the cab's rear-view mirror.

"Never fear! Compared to traffic in Cairo, this is nothing!" Hussein said loudly, weaving through traffic at alarmingly high speeds. Even though I was exhausted, his daredevil driving shocked me into being wide awake.

"Where have you been?" Hussein asked.

"Thailand and Japan. I was there to study Buddhism," I replied.

"Those Buddha people—do they believe in God?" he asked.

"It's complicated. It's not like Islam or Christianity. They believe in reincarnation and that we are all energetically connected," I explained.

"The work of Satan!" Hussein bellowed.

"It depends on how you define the devil. They have Mara, the lord of death, who—"

"Ridiculous!" he interrupted. Then he asked, "What religion are *you*?"

"Catholic," I answered.

"Maybe you will go to heaven—maybe you will not!" Hussein exclaimed.

I gasped, wondering if he was about to test that theory as we whizzed around a bus and cut in front of a tractor trailer. I closed my eyes to pray, but in the back of my mind I kept thinking that if I were in a theme park, this would be called Mr. Hussein's Wild Ride.

"The Quran is the one true word of God!" Hussein proclaimed.

I remained silent for the rest of the trip. True to his word, Hussein got me to Newark Airport just in time to catch my flight. As I handed him the fare and a tip, he glared at me again, his huge green eyes blazing. "I will pray you do not go to hell—even though you are an infidel!"

"Gee, thanks," I said as he turned to grab the luggage of another person hailing a taxi.

The next day, I was invited to attend a service at an Orthodox Church. I thought it was a Greek Orthodox Church, but upon my arrival I was informed that it was an Antiochian Orthodox Church. Now in ruins, Antioch was one of the great cities of the ancient Middle East. In the early days of Christianity, many of the first Christians were from Antioch.

The priest presiding over the mass had a very warm and inviting manner, and I noticed the service was very similar to a Roman Catholic mass. After mass, I was invited to a break-fast of fellowship with the congregation. A young man with a thick Russian accent approached me and asked, "What religion are you?"

"Catholic," I told him.

"You are a heretic! The Pope is a false prophet!" he declared.

"Seriously? What is this, the great schism of AD 1054?" I asked, referring to the split between the Greek Orthodox and Roman Catholic Churches during the medieval era.

"You know about that?" he queried, taken aback by this knowledge.

"Yes, and it's been a thousand years! Isn't it time to get over that? We're all Christians here; we are all people of faith," I responded.

"The Catholic Church is Satan's whore," he said.

"Excuse me?" I replied.

"The Church of Antioch is the original and one true Church of God!" he shot back. "Your soul is dark, and because you are a Catholic, you will burn in hell!"

"That's probably not the best way to make people want to join your church," I said as I put down the baklava I was about to eat and left.

Later that day, I was asked to attend a grief support group. I gave a brief presentation on the use of spirit contact as a therapeutic step in the journey through grief. When I finished, a woman stood up, Bible in hand, and said, "You're a Satanist! Mediums are not of God! You're doing the work of the devil! There is only one true way to God!"

"And I'm assuming it is your way?" I asked.

"I believe in the word of God as written in the Bible!" she exclaimed.

"Which version of the Bible?" I asked, unable to contain myself.

"The one true version: the King James Version of the Bible. I suppose you think the Roman Catholic Bible is the true version," she said as she laughed and rolled her eyes.

"Well, then," I responded. "There is the Roman Catholic version of the Bible, but there is also the Greek Orthodox Bible—and I was informed earlier today that the Antiochian Orthodox Bible is the original and one true Bible, and all three of those predate the King James Version by a thousand years."

"You're making this up," she sneered.

"No, ma'am, this is history," I explained. "Martin Luther's version of the Bible was written in German, which prompted King James to order a Bible written in English. Then there's the Russian Orthodox, the Armenian Catholic, and the Coptic Christian Bible of Ethiopia—they're the ones who claim to be keepers of the Lost Ark of the Covenant."

"Is this true?" she sounded puzzled.

"With all due respect, and I truly respect your beliefs, but there are many versions of the Bible. There's the Byzantine Catholic Bible based on the Alexandrine version of the Bible, and it's somewhat different from the Greek Orthodox Bible—and the Bible of the Thomas Christians of India. It is believed that they are descended from the followers of the

Apostle Thomas, known as 'Doubting Thomas,' whose mission supposedly led him to India. These are just a few versions—and each and every one of those people of faith believes their version of the Bible is the one true version," I explained.

"They do?"

My spiritual situational awareness told me a male presence was with her and wanted to lovingly reach out to her. "You're upset because your husband died," I replied. "It's okay to be angry about that."

"How did you know about my husband?" she asked tearfully.

Realizing she was in pain and not quite ready for interdimensional communication from her husband's spirit, I thanked her and everyone for inviting me—and left. The facilitator of the group followed me to the parking lot and explained how the woman had been emotionally devastated since her husband's death, and said, "You just might have gotten through to her."

In the span of twenty-four hours I was called an infidel, a heretic, and a Satanist by three different people who each believed that their way was the one and only way to God. These were not bad people; they simply had strong convictions about their respective faiths, and they have a right to their beliefs.

Yet it never ceases to amaze me how so many people believe their path is the one and only right path to God. When you disagree with them, their response is that you are going to hell and are doing the work of the devil. In short, it's my way or the Hell Highway!

Is there really a devil? Did God actually create a negative entity to fight with for eons to eventually triumph over like a Norse god in a Viking myth? Or is the devil a metaphor for our own internal struggles between positive and negative behaviors and impulses?

ONE OF THE purposes of interdimensional communication is to dispel fear by presenting evidence from the Light. People fear what they do not understand and tend to give this primitive fear a face, which for many is the devil.

Belief in the devil is not only primitive, it contradicts monotheism. It represents faith in a lesser deity that some feel has control over their lives. This belief is premised on giving a negative spiritual entity godlike power. The devil is a convenient scapegoat for frightening people into conforming to a particular dogma, or set of behaviors. Demonizing people who are different and proclaiming as evil what you do not understand isn't faith; it's fear. Faith through fear isn't faith at all; it's coercion and a form of bullying. I do not mean to pass judgment on any faith or religion. It is my belief that religion and faith are essential in one's life. However, all too often religion is manipulated by people to justify anger, bigotry, hatred, and violence.

To find the devil, look within. Everyone has negative feelings and impulses. It's what you do with them that determines positive or negative behavior. The devil is a metaphor for the negative emotions and desires flowing through every person. This is not to say evil does not exist—just reading the news proves that it does. However, people cause these negative behaviors by indulging their negative feelings, impulses, and desires. To cling to negativity is to manifest the devil within. Those who aspire to follow the path of light and overcome these negative feelings, impulses, and desires embrace their connection with God. The internal struggle within between light and dark is essential to spiritual development.

In the gospels of Luke and Matthew, it is described how, after being baptized by his cousin John the Baptist, Jesus went into the desert and fasted for forty days and forty nights. There he was tempted by Satan to forsake his spiritual path and embrace the self-centered path of materialism and indulgence. This was an important event in the life of Jesus and his mission on earth.

Jesus was gifted beyond measure. He had an unparalleled wisdom and intellect. He was a compelling speaker, healer, prophet, intuitive, medium, and teacher. Through his mother, Mary, he was a descendant of King David. In short, if Jesus had pursued earthly desires and materialism, he had the skill, intellect, speaking ability, and regal bloodline to become immensely wealthy or a major political figure. Obviously, Jesus rejected the material path and fulfilled his destiny by embracing his spiritual nature—his Christ Consciousness. According to Edgar Cayce, "Christ Consciousness is the awareness within each soul, imprinted in the pattern of the mind and waiting to be awakened by the will, of the soul's oneness with God."

Jesus showed people the way to this elevated level of consciousness through the examples he set while in human form. Jesus also taught through the use of parables, such as the parables of the good samaritan and the prodigal son. This is why many biblical scholars believe that the temptation of Christ was a parable. It was Jesus's way of explaining the inner experience wherein he rejected material desire and embraced his enlightened spiritual nature.

There is a strikingly similar parable about Buddha. Three hundred years before Jesus came into the material world, Siddhartha Gautama was born in India to a royal family. According to legend, his father, the king, did not want the young prince Siddhartha to know pain and suffering, so he shielded his young son from the tragedies of the world. One day Siddhartha escaped from the royal enclosure and was horrified when he saw poverty, death, and disease.

It is much easier to see Buddha as a peaceful sage than as a disillusioned young prince traumatized by the suffering of the world. Siddhartha's spiritual path led him to go forth into the wilderness. On the way he found a huge tree, which came to be known as the Bodhisattva Tree. For forty-nine days he fasted and meditated beneath the Bodhisattva Tree. While he meditated, Mara, the lord of death, tempted Siddhartha with images of beautiful women and earthly desires.

When Siddhartha ignored these distractions, Mara tried to frighten Siddhartha with armies of monsters. Siddhartha rejected this illusion of fear and continued to meditate. As Siddhartha freed himself from material world desires and fears, Mara faded away. With his mind purified, he became enlightened and was transformed into the Buddha, which means "awakened one."

The root word of enlightenment is *light*. There is one God, and that God is often perceived as Light. All faiths—from Hinduism to Spiritualism—describe God in terms of Light. As I mentioned earlier, in near-death experience studies people who clinically die and separate from their bodies describe meeting loved ones who have died, and then they describe the brilliant Light filled with a profound and loving intelligence. Many near-death experience subjects say it is an encounter with God. Even then, the word *God* is too limiting, as God—the Source, the Great Spirit, the Creator, Allah, Vishnu, Christ, Lord—is so beyond our mortal understanding, and yet the Light is perceived as unconditional love. The Light is our way of glimpsing, if only for a moment, God's spiritual energy.

Perhaps the great spiritual teachers were revealing to us that the Light is also within. Although Jesus and Buddha became enlightened, they also showed us the way to becoming *in*lightened. By rejecting the darkness of negativity within, we become aware of the Light within—our connection to the spiritual energy of God.

The devil is a metaphor for the negative choices we make. The late Flip Wilson was a comedian who developed the catch phrase "the devil made me do it." But did the devil make you do it or did *you* make you do it? The devil is within all of us. Think about when you have done something negative—when you have been rude to someone or when you have harmed another. Were you acting out of love—or were you acting selfishly?

When we behave in a "self as the center of the universe" manner, we are behaving in an egocentric way. We don't need a devil to make us do things that hurt other people. We do them ourselves when we act in a totally selfish manner.

Embracing love and rejecting an egocentric existence is not an easy journey. It takes time, patience, dedication, and self-reflection. When you see beyond yourself, you will find the path to "inlightenment." This is the message Jesus and the other great teachers—Krishna, Buddha, Lao Tzu, Paramahansa Yogananda, St. Francis of Assisi, Gandhi, Martin Luther King Jr., Mother Teresa—taught in their words and through their deeds.

While this is difficult to achieve, there is a shortcut to inlightenment. Follow the Golden Rule, which all religions espouse but for which Jesus is so well known: "Treat others the way you wish to be treated." This is so simple, yet sometimes so difficult.

All of the major religions teach a similar message: that we are more than just a physical body and that we are all children of one God. There are as many potential paths to God as there are people in the world. God exists in spite of religion, not because of religion. We perceive God as Light, and although the lamps may be different, the Light is the same.

THE BENEFITS OF interdimensional communication and understanding messages from the Other Side are countless. In the esoteric sense, it is essential to our spiritual development to acknowledge that living in the material world is merely part of our evolution as an immortal spirit. Philosophically, what we can perceive with our five physical senses is extremely limited. By acknowledging the existence of the Other Side, we broaden our spiritual situational awareness. Over the centuries this idea frightened a lot of religious leaders because it threatened their sect's domination of the "one and only road to heaven" claim. Therefore, demonizing mediums and claiming interdimensional communication as the work of the devil was convenient.

One of the benefits of interdimensional communication is to eliminate fear and replace it with the understanding inlightenment brings. As you begin to see and analyze evidence from the Other Side, it diminishes the fear that death is the end of existence. As much as I intellectually enjoy studying the nature of interdimensional communication and the theories that support its reality, it pales in comparison with the true importance of contact with the Other Side. Leaving aside the esoteric, it may simply be a matter of love.

Interdimensional communication proves that love transcends physical death. It also enables those of us living in the material world to resolve issues with our loved ones in spirit. Resolution helps us heal. Through healing, we let go of the sorrow in our lives so that we can move forward and grow personally, emotionally, mentally, and spiritually.

We're not alone in this quest for inlightenment. Whether one is living in the material world or living on the Other Side, we all have the capacity to be agents of God's will. Spirits play a large part in our personal evolution, and the best part is you're never too old for inlightenment.

This became so clear to me during a reading for an elderly gentleman. His wife of over sixty years had passed nearly a year before. Her spirit conveyed this message: "It's okay to open the window again."

Although it didn't seem noteworthy at first, I felt that I needed to pause before revealing the next sequence of information. I'm glad I did, as this kindly gentleman started to weep.

"My wife died of cancer. It took her months to die. She was so weak she couldn't leave her room. Her one joy was looking out the window next to her bed. She would stand next to the window and lean against the glass to see the garden outside."

I did not interrupt.

"Since she died, I won't let anyone touch the window in that bedroom. When the light hits the glass at the right angle, I can still see her handprint."

This simple message made all the difference in the world to this man.

After the reading, the gentleman and I talked about the complexity of his wife's multiple-meaning message. It wasn't only evidence of her everlasting life in heaven, it was a metaphor for all of us. In our grieving, we may shutter ourselves behind our defenses and close ourselves in, surrounded only by pain. But there comes a time when it is important to open the window again—and to breathe the glorious fresh air of a new phase of life.

Acknowledgments

The greatest gifts in life are your family and friends; I have been blessed with both in abundance. I would especially like to thank my father, Earl, my sister Roxanne, my brother Earl Joseph, and my niece Laura and nephew Earl for always being there for me. Special thanks to my cousin Laurie Fabiano for her amazing and tireless research into our family's Italian ancestry and for her novel *Elizabeth Street*.

Special thanks to my "team": Rocky Trainer, Nancy Gershwin, Marianne Pestana, Ken Elliott, Jules Feiler, R. J. Clanton, Sue Rice, Casey Feldt, Gina Henderson, Melinda Singer, Brian St. Ours, and Troy Ford, along with the whole staff at Ewareness, Mark Lewis and Mike Misconi, and the crew at Tight Line Productions.

I'm extremely grateful for my extended family: Butch and Jan Giessman, Evelyn Tallman and the entire Tallman clan, Dan and Marti Pradel and the entire Pradel family, Nancy and Mel Rowe, Louise Kleba, Roger Pierce, James Goodman, Rev. Scott Elliott, Rev. April Rane, Kelley and Mary Dunn, and Juen Joyce.

Special thanks to my literary agent Jeff Herman. Thank you to Amy Glaser, Becky Zins, Bill Krause, John Absey, Andy Belmas, and the entire staff of Llewellyn Publications.

Thank you to my colleagues Dr. Raymond Moody, Dr. Kenneth Ring, Dr. Jeffery Long, Dr. Joe Vitale, Dr. My Haley, William Buhlman, and Deborah King for your support and guidance.

It would take a book in itself to thank everyone who has worked on my book signings and public events. I would like to thank some of those wonderful people, including Cheri Hart, Jean Haller, Diane Fresquez, Paula Morin, Bill and Beverly Ford, Joe Yurkovic, Karen Harrison, Rosene Compaine, Kaori Fischer, Donna DeTeresa, Victoria and George Ackerman, Chris and Ginger Pennell, Nance Corriveau, Allison Parker Hedrick, and Rev. Marrice Coverson.

Thank you to Deborah Duncan, Michael Smith, Michael Hubberd, and Heather Itzen of *Great Day Houston*. Thank you to George Noory, Lisa Lyons, John B. Wells, Dave Schrader, Tim Dennis, Mallie Fox, Gary Mantz and Suzanne Mitchell, Smoki Bacon and Dick Concannon, Dan Rea, Diana Navarro, Brenda Michaels, Cyrus Webb, Harry Douglas, Rob McConnell, Brian Sullivan, Lisa Kocher and BettyAnne Martino, Bonnie Albers, Bobby Pickles, Brenda Michaels, Cogee, David Barnett, Dick Sutphen, Eddie Mullins, Inez Bracy, Joe Rumbolo, Ken Ballos and Ray "Big Ray" Rucker, Jim Malliard, Philippe Matthews, Vince Daniels, and Scotty Rorek.

I'd also like to thank the "Jersey Gals," Denise, Barbara, Diane, Joanie, and Monica, along with amazing people I've met on my journeys, some of whom are Nancy Peltonen, Michael Racanelli, Jane Chapin, William and Iris Delgado, Ellen Hartwell, Connie Hayes, Shirley Bolstok, Sandra Fabbri, Lori Kleppner, Robert Littlejohn, Marion MG, Traci Anello, Kathy Satterfield, Kathy Ekdahl, Pat Jean Brenda, Dawn Starz, Eileen Ruth, Becky Burton, Marie Picart, Linda Madere, Nancy Hamilton, Renatta Estevam, Michelle Itzel, Ken Burnette, Barbara Lupo, Joanne Mazzotta, Paige Herrin, Masami Kolbensch, Raksha Andreassen, Phyllis J. Fouts Turpin, Dee Thompson, Sharyn Jordan, Karina Vazquez, Peter Loiacono, Shannon Vance, Charles Labate and Ale Sepulveda.

And eternal thanks to my mother, Jeannie, who is my guiding light from the Other Side.

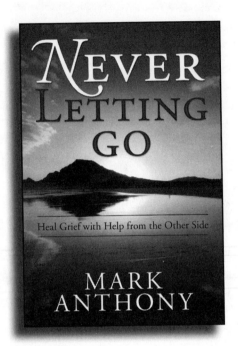

NEVER LETTING GO

Heal Grief with Help from the Other Side

MARK ANTHONY

Never Letting Go

Heal Grief with Help from the Other Side

Mark Anthony

After his mother's death, Mark Anthony was devastated—until he experienced the impossible: a visit from her. This profound and life-changing experience not only helped him cope with crushing grief but inspired him to develop his gift of spirit communication and bring healing to others.

Opening up to the notion that life transcends death is the first powerful lesson in this engaging and uplifting guide to healing from grief. Evidence of the soul's immortality is illustrated in moving accounts of the author delivering life-affirming messages of forgiveness, gratitude, hope, and comfort from loved ones on the Other Side. By sharing his experiences and wisdom as a psychic lawyer and medium, Mark Anthony reveals the healing nature of spirit communication and the rewards of opening our hearts to beloved friends and family in spirit.

978-0-7387-2721-9 • 5³⁄₁₆ x 8 • 288 pages • $15.95

To Write to the Author

If you wish to contact the author or would like more information about this book, please write to the author in care of Llewellyn Worldwide, and we will forward your request. Both the author and the publisher appreciate hearing from you and learning of your enjoyment of this book and how it has helped you. Llewellyn Worldwide cannot guarantee that every letter written to the author can be answered, but all will be forwarded. Please write to:

Mark Anthony
% Llewellyn Worldwide
2143 Wooddale Drive
Woodbury, MN 55125-2989

Please enclose a self-addressed stamped envelope for reply or $1.00 to cover costs. If outside the USA, enclose international postal reply coupon.

Many of Llewellyn's authors have websites with additional information and resources. For more information, please visit our website:

HTTP://WWW.LLEWELLYN.COM